Woody,
    I hope you enjoy this
book and that it will
help make 1995 your best year ever!
        Best wishes,
            Charlie Jewell

COURAGE
TO
LEAD

WOODY COBBS

COURAGE
TO
LEAD

Charlie Farrell

Printed in the United States of America
10 9 8 7 6 5 4 3 2 1

Cataloging in Publication Data

Farrell, Charles E., 1944-
    Courage To Lead/Charlie Farrell
      p. cm.
    I. Title
PS3556.A763C6   1994
813'.54—dc20   94–72677
                         CIP
ISBN: 0–9642047-0-3 (HC)
        0–9642047-1-1 (PB)

BOOKS

104 Rustic Ct.
Columbia, SC 29210

To my daughter, Allison,
whose courage is an inspiration.

ACKNOWLEDGMENTS

A friend read the final draft and after lavishing much praise asked, "Did you have a ghost writer?" My translation: "The book is terrific, but since you, Farrell, aren't possibly smart enough to have written it, who did?"

Well, for better or worse, I wrote it—in longhand, on a legal pad. I dictated it into a micro cassette for Sandra Staub and my wife, Susan, to run through the Mac.

Looking at what I had written, I immediately said, "I need help." So I sent the unedited manuscript to some people I respect and asked for their input: Al Walker, past president, National Speakers Association; Chuck DeVlaming, F-16 flying buddy and attorney in Belleair, Florida; Bill Estabrook, Administrator of Manatee County, Florida; Steve Garris, Director of the Daniel Management Center at the University of South Carolina; Mac Greeley, West Point graduate and Marine Corps pilot, Associate Editor at the Naval Institute in Annapolis, Maryland; Shields Harvey, former President/CEO of one of the country's most successful vending and food service companies; Jim Hawkins, Senior Vice President of the Federal Reserve Bank of Atlanta; Mike Livingston, award winning journalist for Knight-Ridder Newspapers; Connie Mann and Missy Weld, national marketing directors and program developers for The Farrell Group; Andy Sabol, retired training director of the Jacksonville, Florida,

Electric Authority; Bill Holverstott; and Wilson Farrell.

The last two on the list deserve special mention. Bill Holverstott and I started our flying careers together as Marine Corps Lieutenants in Pensacola, Florida. He flew Phantoms in Viet Nam and flew two years with the Navy's Blue Angels. He is presently a 767 Captain with American Airlines. The amount of time and expertise Bill gave was above and beyond the call of duty.

The other is my brother Wilson: engineering graduate from Duke, Navy Officer, and real estate development manager. Two of his greatest assets, significant leadership experience and a passion for literature, combined to make a positive impact on this work.

Getting input from these diverse sources was invaluable. Although I never changed the story per se, their suggestions brought new life to the leadership principles.

Finally, I called in English teachers Dianna Parham and Jo Anne Barrineau to clean up the grammar and punctuation. They were terrific. Dianna's help was exceptional since her input was a mix of editing and proofreading.

Chuck Sookikian, genius with a pen, did the illustrations. My sister-in-law, Suzy Farrell, professional artist with numerous national awards, designed the cover and drew Charlotte's picture. I extend special thanks to my wife, Susan, who ran the computer and never once complained when

I asked late on many nights to make "one last correction." Tom Prince of Edwards Brothers in Ann Arbor, Michigan, gave extraordinary service in the printing.

Where did I learn these stories and principles of leadership? The "anvil" came from Harold Gillespie in Greenville, South Carolina. "Sticks and stones" came from a wonderful speech I heard in Kansas City five years ago from a man whose name I don't know. The rest of it, I don't have any idea. I suppose most of it came from hundreds of different experiences and thousands of clients I have worked with over the years. I have learned a whole lot more from them than they have from me. After all, who knows exactly when we learned about 2 plus 2, the sky is blue, following through on commitments, and saying thank you for a job well done?

I don't claim any of these principles originated with me. As Jack Harden so wisely said, these principles have been around for thousands of years. I only claim the form they are in. If anyone can claim authorship, I will be more than happy to acknowledge it in the next printing.

Finally, I acknowledge you for reading this book. It tells me something good about you—that you are interested in a subject that is vitally important. We are somewhere on a time line in the game of life. If our team is going to win, the leaders in our families, businesses, and government must step forward . . . with courage. I wish you the best.

One

The sign said, "Welcome to Eagle Springs, All-America City." It was cool for a spring day, overcast with the threat of rain. An elderly woman was sitting in a rocking chair on the porch of her neat white frame house. I stopped the car in front, making sure not to drive on the newly-mowed grass. I walked up and asked, "Ma'am, can you tell me how to get to the street where the parade will be?"

"Are you leading it or watching it?"

I was taken aback by her question because I

didn't know it made any difference.

My quizzical expression gave me away as she continued, "The leaders will be gathering in one place, but the watchers will be in another . . . kinda like life, you know."

"Oh, no ma'am, I'm not leading; I'm just watching."

"Well, that's okay, everyone can't lead," she quickly replied with a hint of a smile. "Someone has to be on the sidelines cheering them on. The parade will be coming down Front Street. Go to the second stop sign, take a left and you'll run right into it. Take the first parking spot you come to because there might be a big crowd. When you get down there, you will see a two-story gray building on the right corner. If it's real crowded, go around back and take the stairs up to the roof— your family will have the best view in town. Not many people know about it, so don't spread the word."

I gazed at her for only a second or two, but it seemed she reminded me of someone I knew well from long ago, a person with whom I had felt comfortable.

She was neatly attired in a simple white dress, her bobbed gray hair swept back from her face. On her necklace hung a small, solid gold sand dollar that shone brightly even on an overcast day. It was not the sort of jewelry you see every day in a small town in the heartland of America. She sat erect, not stiff. Her smooth complexion belied the years, and the lines of her face seemed not so much from age, but experience. Her Mediterranean blue eyes and calm voice showed warmth and compassion.

But there was something else, a feeling of strong confidence, maybe even a toughness formed in the crucible of life, that said assertively, *"I have been there, in the arena, in the pit. I have fought the good fight. Although I may not have won in the traditional sense, I have survived. That, under the circumstances, is something I am proud of. If life is a game of king-of-the-hill, then I am on top and you had better pack a very substantial lunch if you think you can get me down."*

First impressions can be deceiving.

My initial thought was that here was little ol' granny waiting on her grandchildren to come over for the usual Saturday morning milk and cookies.

"Thanks so much for your help, and I hope you have a nice day," I told her.

I realized the sun had just come out. It was going to be a beautiful day after all. I also realized that perhaps I just had a brief encounter with a very special person, that this was a woman of substance and experience, the kind of person I would enjoy sitting on the porch with and talking about things that matter.

I returned to the car. The kids were having a pillow fight accompanied by about 100 decibels of noise from their pent-up excitement.

My wife's face said it all—"Let's hurry to the

parade and get these wild hoodlums out of the car!"
We calmed the kids down, I waved a thanks again
to the lady and headed toward the second stop sign.

"What was that all about?" Susan inquired.

"Oh nothing, just an old lady wanting to chat
. . . kinda like life, you know."

Two

here was a big crowd. The two-story gray building with the stairs in the back provided a great view, and there was only a handful of people on the roof. I don't know why I felt special, but I did—like I was in on a secret. The parade was good—if you're into parades. Lots of bands, floats, horses, clowns, the usual parade fare. At any rate, the kids were loving it.

But my mind was on other things, and Susan sensed it.

"What are you thinking about?"

Charlie Farrell

"Work, I guess. A rumor hit the street this week that they're going to lay off, including some managers."

"We've heard those rumors before," she said quietly, brushing little Jake's hair from his eyes.

"I know, but it may be for real this time. The pressure's really intense, and we keep making a lot of costly mistakes that are my responsibility."

"Your career's on track," she said, "so you'll be safe." My last promotion was a big one, but it had put me in the spotlight as manager of a 50-person production department.

"Maybe," I countered, "but I'm just not having fun. Between the technical questions and people problems, I get overwhelmed." I had always considered work fun, sort of a necessary hobby, but lately it seemed I was simply going through the motions.

"Well, let's try to have a nice day," Susan said as she turned back to the parade.

The procession came to a stop as the right rear tire on the Shriners' float went flat right in front of us. A crew of men in funny hats descended on the scene to repair the damage to the tire and their reputation. I had always wondered how long people could march in place. It looked as if I was getting ready to find out as the Chickapee Golden Bears Marching Band majorettes were doing just that in their shiny white boots with gold tassels and with big smiles on their faces . . . for now.

A fellow about my age was standing a few feet

away with his family. We made eye contact and shrugged our shoulders in unison as if to say, "Well, if this is the worst thing that happens all day, we're in good shape." The kids were still wide-eyed and shouting at the clown giving away candy to throw some up to the roof. The clown couldn't hear us, of course, so we didn't get a chance at the candy. Just proves again: for every benefit there's an associated cost.

"You folks from around here?" I asked.

"Yes, we live out on the edge of town in a subdivision called Rolling Wood. How 'bout you?"

"We just came down from Callaway for the day to see the parade—nice community you have here."

"Yeah, we like it. Kinda quiet and small, but close enough to you so we can come up and spend our money," he said, chuckling. As he surveyed the length of Front Street, he said, "Nice view, huh?"

"Great! By the way, what's this parade all about? Is it for some centennial celebration or something?" Susan, a history buff, was always dragging me around trying to educate me.

"Yep, Eagle Springs turns a hundred this year. Just imagine what this street was like in 1923 . . ." he answered.

"I can't believe it's already 2023—seems like just yesterday we were celebrating the turn of the century," I said. "I bet this building was one of the first ones built. Who does it belong to?"

"It belongs to a Mrs. McArthur, or used to,

anyway."

"What does she do?"

"She's retired now. Used to run a business that was owned by her husband who died unexpectedly in his late 30's. It was a small manufacturing company on the edge of town, but nobody wanted the headaches, so she couldn't sell it. She took it over because she had to, really. Her kids were small, and there were no other family members, but she worked hard building the business, was quite successful and later on sold it. This building was her retail outlet, which I think she still owns and rents to the new owners. She's an interesting, tough old bird—kinda keeps to herself. I'm not sure about her health, but the rumor is she did okay on the sale of her business and is living comfortably here in town."

"Do you know her?"

"Not really. I've met her a couple times, but I had a friend who worked for her. He said she was the best manager he's ever seen."

"What does she look like?" I inquired.

"Late fifties, early sixties, gray hair, nice looking lady."

Terrific, I thought, he's only describing every sixty year old woman in America.

"You can always recognize her though. She wears a unique gold sand dollar on her necklace for good luck."

"Enjoyed meeting you," I said. "Looks like the Shriners did their thing, so I guess we'd better get

back to the parade. Have a good day, and thanks
for the conversation."

"Have a safe trip home," he concluded. "Maybe
we'll see you around again."

"Sure hope so."

An Indy 500 pit crew they were not, but with
their vested interest in avoiding 3,000 kids' dis-
content, the Shriners did a quick job on the tire.
The parade resumed, and the Chickapee Golden
Bears Marching Band majorettes, with gold tassels swinging, moved forward with the smiles . . .
still on their faces!

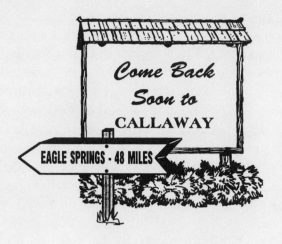

Three

$\mathcal{A}$s always, Monday morning was tough—getting people organized, meeting with managers at 9:00 a.m., calling sales, quality control and personnel. The mail was stacked high, and my worst nightmare—a whole pallet of *our* product on the loading dock with big red letters, "RETURN TO SHIPPER." I certainly understand the concept of running lean and mean, but this was ridiculous.

In the midst of the chaos, I recalled my meeting with Mrs. McArthur when she asked, "Are you

leading the parade, or are you just watching it?"
I thought I knew something about management
and leadership. I had been to all the schools, read
the books and memorized all the conventional
wisdom, but for the first time, her question really
made me wonder: "Am I leading this parade, or
am I just watching?"

Mike Patton, head of quality control, was heading toward my office. I was sure he was coming
to talk about the red letters on the pallet, because
when QC came calling it was never to talk about
the weather. He came into the office and closed
the door behind him. When he saw the look on
my face, he put up both hands, shook his head,
and said, "No, no. I'm not here to talk business."

"Oh, I know, you're here to wish me 'Happy
Birthday.'"

Mike laughed. Then he became serious. He
rubbed his hands nervously as if he had forgotten
the opening line of his rehearsed speech.

"I just wanted to tell you I know you're having
a tough time over here, and if there's anything I
can do to help, let me know."

"That's mighty kind, Mike, I appreciate it."

Mike was one of the good guys. We didn't always agree, but he was fair and never tried to make
himself look good at someone else's expense.

People have either a "can do" or "can't do"
mentality. Although our separate roles led to some
natural disagreements, he was constantly searching for ways to improve production.

"How was your weekend?" he asked.

"Good, we went to a parade down in Eagle Springs."

"How was it?" he asked, appearing genuinely interested.

"It was fun. We met some fascinating people."

"In Eagle Springs? You're kidding."

I told him about my brief encounter with Mrs. McArthur and the conversation with the fellow on the roof.

"She sounds interesting. Maybe we ought to hire her to come up here and get this place squared away. But at her age, she probably doesn't have enough years left."

"You're probably right about that."

Mike had gone to a leadership conference before the training dollars disappeared. Trying to sound casual I asked, "What did you learn at that seminar you went to awhile back? Was it the usual waste of time?"

"It was interesting, but it'd be a lot easier to show you than tell you." He looked out on the production floor. "Look over by machine #4. Let's just watch those people for a while."

After a few minutes, he continued.

"It's obvious the one on the left is the leader, the one on the far right is helping, and the one in the middle is just watching. That's one of the things they told us about leadership: some lead, some follow, and some are the third part of that old saying, 'just keeping the hell out of the way.'"

Charlie Farrell

"Why do you suppose it turns out that way? Why is it that only a few people lead?" I asked.

"Well, some choose to be leaders early on and are doing what comes naturally. Some are thrown into that position against their will. Some think they want the responsibility, but when they finally get it, figure out it's a whole lot harder than they thought and they really struggle.

"There's a theory that people are promoted to their level of incompetence. Just because you can run a machine doesn't mean you can lead other people running machines."

Mike looked at me, and I was wondering if he was referring to me. I had done great in my previous job. But now . . . maybe he thought I was incompetent. Maybe they all did.

I was having some real doubts and fears for the first time about my ability to lead. How much of that was my fault? I was overloaded with problems I really had no control over. I was not getting support from upper management, I inherited some malcontents that were impossible to get rid of, and the economy was on its roller coaster ride down.

"I wonder if that person who is the leader could be a leader somewhere else?" I inquired. What I really wanted to know is whether I could be a leader somewhere else if I couldn't hack it here. I'd had a call from a friend who said his company was looking for a mid-level manager with some manufacturing experience—but he also said something about being shorthanded with an unmotivated work force.

"There's no doubt that leadership skills are transferable," Mike said. "On the other hand, if a person can't lead in one situation, there's no reason to think that individual could lead somewhere else. I guess it's just a question of whether or not someone wants to lead and is willing to pay the price to develop the skills necessary."

"How about technical competence. Where does that come in?"

"Well, you have to know if things are being done right, but it appears, to 'the experts' anyway, that the further along we go, the less technical competence counts. It all gets back to dealing with people. You can know everything there is to know about machinery, but being a mechanic and being a leader are two entirely different things. If technical competence is all it took, your man Lockhart would be running this place."

"Give me a break."

The phone rang. Mike was needed back in his shop. On his way out the door, he said, "One other thing they told us is that if you're in a leadership position, then lead. And if you aren't or can't, then move aside and let somebody else."

I wondered again if he was talking to me or about me.

"Gotta run, Jake. If I can help you, call me. And 'Happy Birthday,' if it is!"

It wasn't.

Charlie Farrell

The rest of the week went pretty much the same. It was one crisis, or as crazy Fred from shipping used to say, one "opportunity" after another. By Friday afternoon, I was ready for the week to end, although it wasn't about to.

Recently I had fallen into that category of people who say, "I sure am glad it's Friday, 'cause I've only got two more days to work this week." I did look forward to Saturdays. I have always been an early riser, so I could get away before the family woke up. I'd go down to the plant, be all alone and knock out a lot of paperwork that I let slide during the week. I asked my wife not to call unless there was a national emergency; I would be home by noon and take the kids out for a burger and a movie, and Susan could go shopping. This seemed to satisfy everybody and became sort of a family tradition.

I thought of my mother-in-law the time I called her on a Saturday morning and asked what she was doing. She gave a hearty laugh and shouted, "Are you kidding me? I'm doing the same thing on Saturday morning I've done for the last 30 years. Henry's playing golf, and I'm washing clothes!" I could only hope that 30 years from now I would not be exclaiming, "Are you kidding me? My family is sleeping in and I am down here, etc., etc., etc."

I headed out on a beautiful Saturday morning. Two lefts and a right, stop at the local greasy spoon for a large cup of black coffee and a gut grenade

Courage to Lead

doughnut; have the same conversation with the waitress, Margie, something like, *"Good morning. The usual? Yes. Have a good day in this good weather/bad weather. Come back to see us. Sure will. Thanks a lot. Goodbye."*

Back in the car, right out of the parking lot, to the light, cross Highway 60, go 4 miles, cross the tracks, turn right, go 3/10 of a mile to the plant entrance on the left. How many times have I made this trip? A bunch. For the first time I asked myself, "How many more times will I make it?" I doubted I would be making this trip much longer.

I got to Highway 60, and the light was red. It was one of those lights that took forever and drove me crazy to catch it red Monday through Friday. But I never minded it early on Saturday, even when I was the only car in sight.

For some strange reason, I felt restless on this particular morning. I could feel my heart beating faster than normal. A little perspiration popped out on my upper lip as I imagined my career slipping away. The weight of this week was particularly heavy, and made heavier by the negative comment my boss made on the way out the door on Friday.

The light changed. I looked in the mirror, no traffic. I couldn't move. For the moment I was paralyzed about my future and my family. My biggest fear in life had always been the fear of failure and here I was on its doorstep without a clue which way to turn. I suddenly remembered a saying from a long time ago: "Insanity is doing the same things over and over and expecting different results."

The light changed again to green. Instead of going straight as I had a thousand times before, I turned left on to Highway 60 and picked up speed. The sign said, "Come Back Soon to Callaway." The sign next to it said, "Eagle Springs, 48 miles."

Four

As I fiddled with the radio, I wondered what I was going to say to Mrs. McArthur. "Hi, I was just in the neighborhood and thought I would . . . uh, I just wanted to thank you again for . . . uh." Maybe I ought to just tell the truth: "I am in some deep, serious trouble with my job, and I was told you were a great manager. I want you to tell me something in the next 5 minutes that will make me the world's greatest leader." That shouldn't be too much to ask; I'll take a few notes, go to work Monday morning, and everything will be fine.

Probably what I ought to do is turn this car around, go back to work, do what I'm paid to do, and stop these hallucinations that some old lady with a gold sand dollar around her neck can tell me anything I don't already know. Besides, what if there's a national emergency, like running out of milk, and my wife does call? What will I tell her? "I just wanted to thank her again?" Right! Talk about cost/benefit. The cost of this little trek in embarrassment alone could be unlimited, while the benefits were unknown at best.

As I passed a slow-moving pick-up loaded with fruit and vegetables, I was thinking maybe she won't be there and this whole episode will pass unnoticed—another one of my great ideas gone south. I guess what I was really afraid of was that I would be disappointed to find out she's not all I hoped she would be. So often, I've been disappointed by becoming emotionally involved with the possibilities of a win/win relationship, only to realize the other person did not share my passion, my values, or my work ethic. This time I would go in with my guard up—hoping for the best, prepared for the worst.

I passed through the little town of Wagner, population 1,420. Three old men in blue jeans were drinking coffee, sitting outside a cafe. They waved at me as if I were an old friend. It always intrigued me that you get that in the small towns, but never in the big cities.

Although my first meeting with Mrs. McArthur was only momentary, there was something very special about her that gave me a spark, made me want more. Her brief comments caused me to think about things I hadn't thought about in a long time. They were a wake-up call about some issues I could not ignore any longer.

I needed help, and I was willing to go anywhere and talk to anyone about it.

I have heard about mentors, but I realize now I never really had someone to go to and ask for help. There is certainly no one at work, my boss least of all. He's stuck in a rut three years from retirement and just marking time.

The plant manager is a nice guy and very helpful, but not what anyone would consider a strong manager. He came down from corporate headquarters a year ago. No one can figure out what he did to deserve the job, but he's got it. He hasn't done anything great; on the other hand, he hasn't done anything real bad either.

Corporate, in effect, has said don't spend a nickel unnecessarily, no extra bodies, don't train, don't invest, make as much money as you can, make the bottom line look good so we can sell. I think he would like to help, but he just doesn't have the clout.

I pulled up to the front of Mrs. McArthur's house, and there was no one in sight. Good, I thought, this lets me off the hook. I pulled into her driveway to turn around. Just as I stopped the car and placed my hand on the gear shift to go into reverse, she turned the corner from the back of the house and came straight up the driveway toward me. She had a handful of flowers and wore coveralls, gloves and a floppy hat. She appeared to recognize me and gave out a cheery, "Hello again!" Putting down her flowers, she continued up the driveway. I put the car in park, cut off the engine and got out.

"Good morning! Did you enjoy the parade?" she cheerfully asked.

"Yes ma'am, we had a great time, and I really appreciate your help. We watched from the building you told us about, and the kids absolutely loved it. You were right, it was the best view in town."

There was an awkward silence as the moment of truth had arrived.

"I guess you're wondering why I'm here. You said something about leadership last week that started me thinking. I want to talk with you further if you have a few minutes."

She responded with a quick smile. "I think I can spare a few minutes. I was looking for an excuse to take a break anyway."

She took off her gloves and extended her hand. "I'm Charlotte McArthur."

"I'm Jake Howe. Nice to meet you, Mrs. McArthur."

In an instant she changed. She seemed to study my face and appeared almost startled. It was as if, like me, she thought she knew me from before and had lost touch over the years. Or maybe she was processing my name through her cranial rolodex trying to match it with one from the past, somewhat embarrassed not to be able to peg it right away.

Her hand was trembling slightly as she touched the gold sand dollar. Her voice remained calm.

"The first rule is that you call me Charlotte. I'm not your boss, and besides, 'Mrs. McArthur' makes me feel old, a stage of life I'm not participating in. Come up on the porch where we can relax," she offered warmly.

There was no way I was going to say I already knew her name, about her husband, her company, her kids and the commercial property she owned. She might find it hard to believe I got all that information from a stranger whose name I don't even know.

"I don't know that I know enough about anything to help you," she continued, settling into her rocking chair. "But I will be more than happy to share with you what I can. First of all, tell me a little about yourself, where you came from, what you're doing now, about your family, and why you're interested in leadership.

"Since I'm not trying to hire you, I guess I can ask you anything I want, right?" she said with a chuckle.

"Right, and since I'm not trying to get a job with you, I might as well tell the whole truth."

"Fair enough," she said, nodding. "Where did

Charlie Farrell

you grow up?"

"I was born in Kansas. My mom died when I was five. My dad was a mid-level executive with a big insurance company. He transferred a couple times, and we ended up in Virginia."

"Did you go to college?"

"Yes. I got a degree in engineering from Virginia Tech."

"What did you do after that?"

"I took a job with Owen Industrial and have been with them ever since."

"What's your product, and what's your job?"

"I'm production manager. We make computer hardware, 3 shifts, very high tech equipment, lots of robotics."

"I see. Where do you live?"

"We live in Callaway. You saw my family—wife, Susan, two children, Jake and Allison, ages 6 and 9. I guess I'm living the American Dream—wife, two kids, a job, two cars, big mortgage, small savings account and, I almost forgot, a Border Collie named Sporty."

"Is your son a junior?"

"Yes, Jacob Riggins Howe. Riggins was the family name on my mom's side."

"And?"

She knew there was more, a whole lot more. It was in my eyes, my voice, my body language. Maybe it was intuitive for her that when she was around someone desperate, she just knew. I felt I was in Times Square in my underwear, all alone, with everybody looking. I was embarrassed, and I didn't know what to do next.

I was thinking there's no reason to hold back now. I'd come this far, but I was looking into the abyss and the jackals were closing in fast. I could either turn tail and run or take a leap of faith and spill my guts and hope that she might know something, say something that would help.

So I took the risk. I told her about the work, the rumors, my boss, my employees, the pressure and how it affects my work. I shared with her how it had adversely impacted my personal life. I told her about my fear for my job, my future, my family; that all three were in jeopardy, and I had doubts about my ability to keep it all together.

Then there was silence. There were no birds singing, no crickets, no cars, no kids. It was the kind of silence that was deafening, where I could hear my own heart beating.

She looked deep into my eyes as if to say, "I not only can see your eyes, but I can read your soul."

Five

She took off her floppy hat, sat way back in her wicker rocker and took a deep breath. Then, calmly she said, "Let me tell you about two events that happened a long time ago, probably just before you were born, if I am guessing correctly, about the late eighties, early nineties. I'm not getting into the details because they're not important. These events occurred simultaneously but were unrelated and took place thousands of miles apart.

"First there was a fellow who was beaten pretty

badly by some people who were supposed to be leaders in the community. Just by chance, someone videorecorded the incident. It was shown on TV over and over, and a big deal was made out of it. Well, the people in the local community were so incensed over this and the subsequent trial, they went on a rampage, destroyed a lot of property, and hurt a lot of people. I, like a lot of people, was greatly disturbed by this.

"The other event took place during the same time frame, but over a longer period of time. A group of men and women, supposedly leaders, were entrusted with our country's finances. Well, unbeknownst to most people, these folks were not doing what they said they would. They allowed practices which were unwise, even criminal. There was no accountability since these people were making up their own rules as they went along. Well, when it all collapsed, a lot of innocent people got hurt. Some people never recovered, and it cost the country billions of dollars to bail it out."

She paused for a second and then said assertively, "So what's the connection?"

In four words her tone completely changed from simply telling a story to one of deep conviction. The lines of her face became sharp. Her eyes narrowed. She leaned forward, as if to say, *"What I am getting ready to tell you is important. These events had a major impact on me, and I am going to give it to you straight up—no icing, no bells and whistles, so pay close attention."*

Courage to Lead

"Very simply," she continued, "both cases could have been avoided. I told you about the TV coverage of the fellow being beaten. I saw it maybe 50 times, and I don't watch much TV. Each time I saw it, I got more upset. Sure, it was terrible what they did to that man, but there was something more subtle than the raw violence that disturbed me. There was something I saw, but didn't understand right away.

"Then it hit me as I watched this thing for about the umpteenth time. While some of the people were beating this guy, there were about 10 others standing there watching—just watching! Any one of these 10 could have stepped in there early on and said, 'OK, that's enough, I'm taking charge of this. You folks are dismissed, see you tomorrow.' But no, they stood there and watched."

"Why didn't they stop it?" I asked.

"Why? Because there was not one person there who had the courage of a leader. Not one damn person was willing to put it on the line in front of their peers and say, 'This is wrong and it will stop!' I could never explain to you the horror of the aftermath of all this. The notes in the history books could never capture the ugliness, the massive destruction of property and the loss of human life. Lives were irrevocably changed for the worse, and it all could have been avoided by just one person with courage."

She put her gloves on the porch railing and continued.

Charlie Farrell

"As the second incident unfolded, it was perfectly obvious the same principles were present. It could have been avoided. People with the courage to lay it on the line could have stopped the greed and deceit, since anyone with a conscience would have known what they were doing was wrong and it wouldn't work in the long run. It didn't take a brain surgeon to figure right from wrong.

"It was," she snapped, "a combination of basic economics and business ethics."

Her tone and manner softened, becoming almost parental.

"First and foremost," she counseled, "leaders have to have courage. You said there were some things going on in your company that you didn't like, that were wrong. There is a big difference between things you don't like and things that are wrong, so you had better get in your mind which is which. You can voice disagreement over things you don't like, but the things you know are wrong you must go to war over. A leader has the courage to say, 'This is wrong.' You have to decide—and I suggest you do it soon—if you have the courage to be a leader, or are content to be a follower, or will stand on the sidelines cheering.

"And by the way, there's no right or wrong choice. There is room, and in fact, a need, for all three because business is like a parade. You need leaders, followers, and folks on the sidelines cheering. You might be a good follower, content just to be told what to do and when to do it."

She waved at a neighbor walking by.

"You mentioned your frustration with some of your employees punching the clock three seconds before start time and not one second after quitting time. You can do that too. No responsibilities, just come to work and do your job, nothing more. With no Saturdays to work, you could sleep in, get up with the kids, and watch cartoons.

"And vacations, you'll never miss a day of vacation—guaranteed! Bad product? So what? You still get paid, it's just a cost of doing business. So what if the company goes bankrupt? There's always a job at the next plant down the road, especially for someone with your high-tech skills. Just look in the morning paper. I guarantee you that in the want ads there is a company close by looking for someone to come in, take over a machine, and put in 40 without complaint. Although the boss might like to have some suggestions from a smart guy like you on how to do better, it is not required. Nobody on a production floor has ever been terminated for not making suggestions.

"You know the biggest benefit of all—you'll never have to see your house in the dark. I never paid much attention to this until one of my plants died."

She pointed out toward the street.

"It was one I planted right out there by the mailbox. I came home early one day and saw it had died. I suddenly realized I hadn't seen my yard in the daylight for two weeks."

She laughed out loud. "Darned expensive plant, too! Yes, you could go to work in the daylight and always be home before dark," she said, wistfully.

She stood up, walked to the edge of the porch and picked a leaf out of a plant. "If you want to be a leader, then there's a little different story. You know that. Already there is no shortage of effort on your part; the fact that you came back here today tells me that.

"But there are some other questions: Do you have the courage to endure criticism and second guessing, problems with no apparent answers, long hours, uncertainty, and the fact that in most cases your job can be terminated in a heartbeat with no recourse? Can you put it on the line for your people? Can you psychologically handle the risk of failure? Just as dying is a part of living, the chance of failure is a part of the success of a leader."

She sat back in her rocker.

"However, failure won't be fatal. It may set you back, but it might also be one of your best learning experiences. And I absolutely do not subscribe to the theory that you have to fail a few times in order to succeed. Maybe those who fail just try the wrong things first, and those who succeed try the right things first. A whole lot is made of Edison and his 10,000 experiments before he invented the light bulb. Well, maybe it was just luck. Maybe if he had tried the right one first, we

would have never had this great story about per-
severance."

"I have to admit that my biggest fear in all of
this is the fear of failure," I offered.

"Well, failing should not be your biggest fear.
If you go through life only doing things to keep
from failing, I am convinced you will not do those
things you need to do to succeed. Thoughts drive
our actions. If there were ever two trains of thought
on the opposite ends of the spectrum, they are 'keep
from failing' versus 'trying to succeed.' The former will keep you safe, out of harm's way and
make you feel secure. The other is very risky. Real
leaders only think in terms of trying to succeed.
They know the risks, but they don't dwell on them.

"The difference is courage."

With this strong statement, Charlotte stood up
slowly, and appeared emotionally drained.

"I'm sorry, I have to go now; I'm a little tired.
Think about these things and if you have the courage to be a leader come back anytime and we'll
talk. If I don't see you again, I wish you the best
of luck. Just don't sit on the fence; either throw
your hat in the ring or put it on your head and
walk away."

She extended her right hand warmly, and with
her left, held the gold sand dollar.

On my way back to Callaway, I could not believe how the time had flown by. She was open
and straightforward with a very quick mind. She
would listen intently and then process the infor-

mation like a high-speed computer. If ever there was a classic case of "nothing beats experience," she was it.

Her wisdom was not acquired from reading books; she had to have lived it. When asked a question, she never rolled her eyes as if thinking, *"What does the book say is the proper response to this?"* Her thoughts came directly from her experience, "I had a situation like that once and what I did was . . .," and it all made sense.

I only hoped that listening to her was not like taking a drink of water from a fire hydrant where only a little gets in and most of it splashes off. I couldn't wait 30 years to learn; I had to do it in a hurry. Life to me was one roll of the dice. If I could get the support of my people and a little help from top management, it might work out. If I couldn't, maybe I could call my friend and see if I could help him with his shortage of technicians. Besides, I hadn't seen my yard in the daylight for a long time, and when I thought about it, the idea sounded pretty good.

I went straight home and shared with Susan my experience and the advice Charlotte had given. She was excited for me since she knew I had been searching a long time for some guidance. Susan asked if I would return the next week. I could tell she was hoping I would.

JAKE
HOWE
LEADER

Six

Charlotte had told me Monday morning would be no different. There were going to be no fewer problems, but maybe I would start to see some things in a different light. There is no quick fix.

On the way to work, I got stopped by a train. As I listened to the cadence of steel wheels on chrome colored rails, it caused me to reflect on a portion of our conversation.

"Becoming a leader is like a train," she said. "When it's moving down the track at full speed, it is a powerful force and is hard to stop. But right now, Jake, you are still in the station at a dead stop with the engine idling. And it won't go from a dead stop to full speed in an instant."

"How long will it take?" I asked.

"Becoming a leader takes time," she said. "Patience and persistence."

"I certainly have no problem with persistence, but patience has not been one of my virtues."

"That's because you were born and brought up in an era of instant gratification, the 'give it to me now generation.' A little impatience is admirable because it supports determination, but leaders are able to harness that urge by realizing there are some things you just can't push.

"What is your favorite cake?" she asked, taking me off guard.

"Black Forest with whipped cream."

"Well, let's suppose you took all the ingredients for Black Forest cake, put them in a bowl and stirred it up. Is it a cake?"

"Of course not."

"It's going to take time to make a cake, just the proper amount—not too little, not too much."

"Do you think I have the right ingredients?" I asked, hopefully.

She didn't hesitate.

"Every person has the right ingredients. If you mix them in the proper amount and give it time, you can be a leader. The only question is whether you want to be a leader. Do you have the courage to make the effort?"

I didn't know if I missed it or if she never got around to saying, but she did mention there is one ingredient that is absolutely essential. I was sure she would tell me next time.

The train passed, and I continued on, my mind shifting quickly to work.

Charlotte was absolutely right about something else, too. Monday morning was no different. Same song, different verse. As for seeing things in a different light, I had the feeling on this Monday morning that the light I saw at the end of the tunnel was simply a big train coming straight toward me.

At about 11:00 a.m., I did see one of my rays of light.

Bill Markston was walking straight toward my office with, as usual, a big smile on his face. Now, here is what leadership is all about. Twenty-seven years old, efficient, effective, loyal, hard-working, always early. As a matter of fact, I asked Betty, our personnel manager, where she got this guy. If I could just get one more person with an attitude like his, I would have it made. She just smiled the smile that said, "Forget it, big boy. The next one I find like him is coming to work for me, not you."

Bill's philosophy of work is to do whatever it takes—early, late, weekends, holidays. He will change shifts on short notice, doesn't matter; just tell him what you want and you've got it. He's

Charlie Farrell

very family-oriented, too, with a wife and two small children. I guess he's been here about a year now. Oh man, time does fly.

I will never forget the first week he was here. When he came in the door, he would go immediately to the nearest trash can and put scraps of paper in it. I thought he was just a "neat freak," keeping his car clean. Then one day I saw him coming across the parking lot, eyes glued to the ground sweeping back and forth like a radar screen and picking up trash along the way.

He stuck his head in the door and cheerfully said, "Good morning, how was your weekend? I came down Saturday morning and couldn't believe you weren't here. First time in history; I'll record that for the archives. You must have had a million-dollar deal going."

"As a matter of fact, I did."

Bill would drop in every once in a while on Saturday on his own time and offer his help, and most of the time I would be there. In fact, we got a lot of work done on those Saturday sessions.

"You know I'm coming up on my first-year anniversary," Bill said, grinning. "Can you believe it? The handbook says I get one week of vacation, so I'm gonna hold you to it. I'm taking my family to the lake for some camping and fishing. Boy, are they excited! I haven't seen the vacation schedule, and I was wondering when . . ."

"I can't believe it, Bill, I should have had that out already. Tell you what, I'm real busy right now; please check with me Friday about noon and I'll have it for you," I said apologetically.

As Bill turned to leave, he responded enthusiastically. "Great, I appreciate that. I'll tell my family, and we will spend this weekend planning our vacation together. See you Friday around noon."

What a guy. If I could bottle that enthusiasm and energy and sell it, I wouldn't have to work here anymore.

I sure hope I didn't give the impression to Charlotte that I disliked or was having problems with *all* of my people because I'm not. Not many are terrific like Bill, but most are solid people I can depend on to put in a good day's work. However, those other few are troublesome. The old 80/20 rule is still alive and well—80% of the problems are caused by 20% of the people.

The phone jarred me back to the next "opportunity" at hand. If I could juggle rubber balls like I have to juggle this job, I wouldn't be on the sidelines at the parade next year, I'd be leading it.

The rest of the week was the same. Even the robot we named Hannibal took a walk on his own. However, I did have a little time to think about some things, and maybe I did see them in a different light. There is a difference between the things I dislike and the things that are wrong, and I found myself focusing on how I could fix the wrong things. She said you could fix only so many things,

Charlie Farrell

so focus on a few. You certainly can't go to war over everything or people will be confused about what is really important.

At about five minutes before noon on Friday, I finished talking to Production Control, and I had another appointment at 12:30 with Human Resources on the revised benefit package. I figured I'd better run down to the cafeteria and grab a sandwich. Lunch "hour" is some more business fiction that I've never experienced.

As I pulled my door, Bill Markston was pushing. There he stood with that big old smile, saying, "I'm here to get the vacation schedule."

"Holy smokes, Bill, I can't believe it. I completely forgot about it."

Totally embarrassed, I continued. "Between the weather, Hannibal, the computer down and two people out sick, it just completely slipped my mind. I really am sorry, Bill, I just completely forgot."

Bill's smile quickly faded to a look of disappointment. I tried to recover lost ground. "I promise I will have it for you first thing Monday, or better yet, if you are coming down tomorrow, I'll have it for you then."

"No, that's okay," he responded quietly. "I'll just get it Monday. Have a good weekend."

"You, too." I could tell he was disappointed, but I'm also sure he understood, more than anyone, what a hectic week it had been. Most of all, he knew my intentions were good.

Friday, 5:00 p.m. I bet if there were a fire at

Courage to Lead

2:30 p.m. on Tuesday, this place would not clear out as fast as it does at 5:00 p.m. on Friday. The parking lot looked like the start of the Le Mans. By 5:10 p.m., it looked as if the plant had been abandoned 10 years ago. Eerily quiet.

I remained with old Hannibal, my sole companion, just standing there. He's kinda neat: doesn't complain, works hard, never late, and about 99.9% perfect. Every once in a while he takes off on his own, like this week, when he deposited some garbage in the Quality Control office. They think we program him to do that when they reject some parts, but I swear we don't. They're pretty close to having these guys thinking on their own. Hannibal may have figured out the ongoing battle between QC and Production and is taking some things into his own hands.

I was starting to think about tomorrow morning and whether or not I should return to Eagle Springs. She said *if* I had the courage to be a leader and wanted to discuss some things, come back any time. But if she didn't see me again, she wished me the best of luck. She did not invite me to drop in anytime for any reason. She said *if* I had the courage to be a leader, come back, and if she didn't see me again . . . pretty easy translation. In this segment of her life, she wanted to deal with me only if I had the courage to be a leader. If I didn't, then I shouldn't bother to come back. No icing on that cake. It was obvious that she has a remarkable passion for leadership and believes courage is the cornerstone.

I recalled what she told me about the day her husband, Wilson, died.

"My kids were taking a nap and I was cooking dinner when the minister arrived. It was a cold and rainy day two weeks before Christmas."

"Did you know anything about the business?" I asked.

"No, not a thing. Wilson was from the old school and frequently said, 'I'll run the business; you run the house.'"

"Did that suit you?"

"It was working out. Wilson was working long hours, but he was committed and happy. And I was happy, too. My master plan was to get the kids up and away and then go work with him part-time or as a nurse's assistant. I always thought about being a nurse."

"Had you ever worked in a hospital?"

"I was a candy striper in high school and a nurse's assistant here at Lincoln Memorial. As a matter of fact, that is where I met Wilson. I was working one Saturday when he came in from a hiking accident. He had fallen down a bank and got a big splinter right in the fanny. He was a tough guy and it didn't hurt, but he was sure embarrassed. I'll never forget the charity ball we attended. Someone in our group said something about an acquaintance being a pain in the rear. Wilson looked at me and laughed so hard tears came to his eyes."

"What did you do after the funeral?"

"Well, I was in a mess. I had not worked outside the home since the kids were born, and I had no formal education. There was a huge mortgage on the house and the business. I made a couple of calls about selling the business, but with the debt and being in a recession at the time, there was absolutely no interest."

She stopped for a few seconds, painfully recalling what must have been a frightening time.

Subdued, she continued.

"About a week after the funeral, just before Christmas, I went into the children's room and looked into their soundly sleeping faces. The one thing they wanted Santa to bring they could never have.

"I sat on a chair between their beds and looked at the curtains I made from cloth we got at a flea market. I looked at the nightstand Wilson had made from scrap lumber. I thought about this home and how hard we had worked to build it. I also knew it was all in jeopardy, and it was up to me. I had no family to turn to.

"I don't know why it hit me like it did, but at that moment I made a promise to my girls that I would not lose this house. I may die in the process, but I would never give up. If I couldn't learn to run the business, I would close the doors and get three jobs, but nobody would say I didn't try. They would never, ever take my home."

"What did you do after that?"

With her strong will evident, she continued. "It was a Sunday night. I called Sherman Stewart, who was my husband's right-hand man. I told him I was going to take the girls to the shore for a couple of days and would be in Wednesday morning to start the management training program."

"What did he say?"

"He just laughed and said he would design it while I was gone. But he also said there would be a lot of people pulling for me. And there were. They were wonderful . . . they are wonderful."

She wiped a tear, regained her composure, and concluded, "Jake, please excuse me, but you're the first person I ever shared that story with."

I was overwhelmed by her story and even a little ashamed of myself. What was the worst thing that could happen to me—that I would lose my job and go work someplace else? With my education and training, it was true, I could get a job with no problem. I'm not in danger of losing my home, and I have a great wife taking care of our kids who is willing to find a job if necessary.

But all that was missing the point. I want to be a leader. Someone once said that what you want written on your tombstone says a lot about what you should do. I want my tombstone to say I was a leader. I also seek responsibility. Like the great athletes in crunch time, I want the ball. I want to run my own show someday.

I don't want to go to work at 8:00 a.m., take an hour for lunch, and be home by 5:15 p.m., run over by the start of the Owen Industrial Le Mans. I can never be satisfied with less than the challenge of leadership.

I would love to watch cartoons with my kids on Saturday morning. I love my children and if it ever works out that I can spend that kind of time with them, great. But if that is one of the sacrifices that I have to make, so be it. I know that Susan will always be there for them even when I cannot. I also realize that time spent working hard, developing my leadership skills, would enable me to spend more time with them in the future.

I knew I had the desire. If I died trying, then my tombstone could say, "He died *trying* to be a leader," but that was okay, too. I was not giving up. I would not do whatever I could; I would do whatever it took. I would spare no time or expense to learn what I needed. My engine may have been just idling, but the engineer threw a big shovel of coal into the furnace, and the pressure started rising.

I would be in Eagle Springs bright and early Saturday morning.

Seven

I love reading about the Old West, especially stories of courage and sacrifice of the pioneers who settled places with romantic names: Cody, Boulder, Yuma, Cheyenne, and Santa Fe.

On my drive to Eagle Springs, I felt like a wagon master on a Conestoga heading west from St. Louis. I was excited but apprehensive about the unknown territory, fraught with danger. I was 300 miles out, past the point of no return, totally dependent on a stranger who came on board at the last moment to navigate the wilderness.

Charlotte was sitting in her rocker. There was a small pitcher of orange juice and some hot-out-of-the-oven and out-of-this-world-smelling coffee cake on a small serving cart. I could smell it as I approached the porch.

As I climbed the steps, she stood up, smiled, and asked the question, already knowing the answer, "Well?"

"I want to lead," I said assertively.

With the biggest smile I had seen so far, she exclaimed, "I knew you would! Let's talk. Tell me about your week."

I told her. She never asked a question, never said a word. She just listened as I relayed everything from early Monday to late Friday—the good, the bad, and the ugly. When I finished she just looked at me. I knew what she was thinking. *Why did I ever get into this? This guy is hopeless. I ought to just shoot him and put him out of his misery.*

Finally, she said, "You mentioned this young fellow and the vacation schedule."

"Yes, Bill Markston," I replied.

"Did you say he is your best employee?"

"Yes ma'am."

"No 'ma'ams'."

"Yes."

"He is your most loyal employee?"

"Yes."

"He is efficient, effective, hard working and

never late. In fact, he's never missed a day of work, right?"

"Yes."

"He comes in on Saturday on his own time. Very family-oriented. Would do anything for you. Anything."

"Yes."

"And you looked that young man in the eye and said that you *forgot* about him and his family's vacation."

I couldn't respond. Suddenly the back of my neck turned into a huge knot, and my mouth went dry. She had a way of asking a question for which no response was necessary or wanted. Her solemn stare was boring a hole right through me.

"Jake, do you read much?"

"Not as much as I should." It was another one of the loves of my life that had recently disappeared.

"Did you ever read a book called *The Right Stuff* by Tom Wolfe?"

"No, I can't say I ever did. What's it about?"

"It's about pilots and astronauts in the early days and what it took to be one. I have often thought that leaders have something called the right stuff. My definition of the right stuff is doing what you say you are going to do, following through on your commitments, all the time—not some times, or most times, but *every* time. If you tell a customer you will call at 2:00, you call at 2:00—not five after, not ten after, not the next morning. You call at two o'clock because that is what you said you were going to do. If you tell an employee that you will have the vacation schedule for him by Friday at noon, it will be there by Friday at noon and not one minute later. If you tell a child that you will go for a walk together in the park on Saturday, you go for a walk in the park on Saturday.

"People who have the right stuff understand three important words in life: *credibility, reliability, and integrity*. I hope those three words mean something to you, Jake, because that is all you really have to offer."

I fidgeted and looked at my hands, knowing that I had never made a connection between leadership and my ability to deliver a vacation schedule on time.

"Jake, what would you say is your company's primary product?"

"Computer hardware."

"I don't think so," she asserted. "And if you ever once think that's what you're selling, you are heading down the wrong road. What you are selling is the credibility, reliability, and integrity that back up that product or service. And I'll tell you what, the day your customers disassociate those three words from your name, you will be on the street. There will be a big padlock on the door, and you will be down at the local pizza parlor looking for a job.

"On a personal level," she concluded, "your credibility, reliability, and integrity are based on one thing, and that is the honest and fair commitments that you make to people and whether or not you follow through."

A squirrel was perched on a tree limb a few feet away. As he cocked his ears and swished his tail, he almost looked sympathetic to this tongue-lashing I was deservedly receiving.

"Have some orange juice," she offered.

Her tone had softened.

"I squeezed it myself on a little contraption we bought on a trip to Florida a long time ago. We stopped at one of those juice stands. The fellow running that thing was a real character; claimed to be a Seminole Indian whose family lived in the Okefenokee Swamp. That guy was from Hackensack, New Jersey, if my name is Charlotte. He roped those tourists in by the dozens, including yours truly. Funny thing is, the juicer still works 25 years later."

She became serious again.

"You mentioned something about a part not being shipped to a customer because somebody forgot, and the customer was upset. Customers put food on the table, and you are telling me that somebody forgot. There is no excuse for that, absolutely no justification.

"One of the worst phrases in the English language is 'I'm sorry, I forgot.' Because when you say 'I'm sorry, I forgot,' you are really telling your customers, your employees, your family and your co-workers, 'I don't care.' That is the underlying message that you send. You are saying, 'I don't care enough about you and the commitment that I made to you to write it down in an organized fashion to ensure that I will follow through.

"One day in our retail store a customer came in—a regular customer named Judy Montgomery. She was terrific, never asked price, never hassled us, and paid her bills promptly. If we could have had a hundred customers like her, we would've had it made. Well, she asked one of our customer service people for some information on a new product she had heard about. Our rep was real busy, thank goodness, but said he did have some information we had just received from one of our suppliers. He told her he would look it up and call her back by the end of the day. Judy said, 'Great, I really appreciate that, and I look forward to hearing from you.'

"Two weeks later I happened to be in the store, talking with the customer service rep about how things were going when Judy walked up. I'll never forget this as long as I live. She said good morning to me and then turned to the customer service rep and asked, 'Oh, by the way, did you get the information I asked for a couple weeks ago?' The young man looked her right in the eye and said, 'I'm sorry, I forgot.' I could have died, and I could have killed a customer service representative to go along with me. He said to the most loyal customer we had, 'I'm sorry, I forgot.' In effect he said, 'We don't forget about the things where we make money off you, but all these other things . . .' There's no excuse for that.

"Jake, does your company spend a lot of time and money on marketing and selling?"

"A tremendous amount."

"Well, in our business we didn't talk a lot about marketing and selling. We talked a whole lot about building relationships. We knew if we built relationships, we didn't have to worry as much about marketing and selling. The problem is that relationships are hard to build, and building them takes a long time. Relationships are like those stamps you get at the grocery store; they go in the books that you redeem for gifts . . ."

I interrupted. "Yes, my wife collects those and guess who gets to lick 'em, one at a time."

She laughed.

"It's nice to see you've been trained correctly. Well, that's what relationship building is all about, one stamp at a time. You build that relationship. You build it and build it and build it. But when we let people down, be they customers, clients, co-workers, family members or friends, it's like ripping a whole page of stamps out of the book, throwing it in the trash can and starting back at square one.

"Relationships are like those stamp books in another way, too. As an example, what would you have done last week if Bill had been five minutes late one day?"

"Nothing," I replied. "He's never been late a single day and is the best employee I have."

"You see, he has built up a huge number of stamps over the past year, so he can expend a few without harm. However, you just threw a whole page of stamps away in your relationship with Bill. The question is, how many stamps did you have to begin with? From what you have told me about his reaction, perhaps you didn't have a surplus account. Maybe there have been other times when you let him down."

"That's true, but my intentions were good," I said defensively.

She smiled.

"Have some coffee cake. I don't cook a whole lot any more. It's not much fun to cook for one, so it's nice to have a reason to get in the kitchen and create something. This was my husband's favorite. You might ought to stop by and see your waitress friend though, 'cause she might forget about you and give your favorite stool to the mailman. Of course, as soon as I tell you all I know, which won't take a whole lot longer, there'll be no reason to come here anymore. Then you can get back to work and start spending your time wisely."

She winked, which she usually did when something rather heavy was getting ready to follow.

"You mentioned your intentions were good. I came face to face with a concept when I was just a little bit older than you that has had a major impact on the way I think, and hopefully on the way I do business. That is knowing the difference between actions and intentions. See, you judge yourself by your intentions, but you are judged by your actions. Now I am sure that your intentions were to get Bill the vacation schedule. You care, you try to do right by your people, is that fair to say?"

"Yes."

"When you said, 'I'm sorry, I forgot,' your thought process was, 'but my intentions are good, so it's really okay.' See, that's how you judge yourself, by your intentions. But how were you judged?"

She didn't wait for my reply.

"I'll tell you how you were judged." Her voice was at full strength now. She became very animated, pointing her finger straight at me.

"That young man was standing there looking deep into your eyes, thinking, '*I work my tail off for you. You call me any hour of the day or night, on weekends and holidays. You change my shifts without notice, take time away from my family, I come in on my own on Saturdays. I'm breaking my back for you down here, and you are telling me that you forgot about me and my family's vacation.*' That is how you were judged, by your actions."

"I see what you mean, and I know I was wrong, but . . ."

"No 'buts'! Your intentions in life mean absolutely nothing, Jake. Let me say that again, and please pay very close attention. *Your intentions in life are meaningless*. The only things in life that count are your actions. So the trick is to make sure your intentions match up with your actions."

Without fear or even half looking, she swatted a bumblebee that had ventured a little too close.

"People want to be led. You want to be led. You mentioned that you wish you had a strong leader. The key to it all is trust. If your people do not trust you, then you can't be their leader. The way they know they can trust you is that you do what you say you are going to do all the time.

"You can be their manager, but you can't be their leader unless they trust you. See, you manage inventory, accounts receivable, and computer systems, but you lead people. The term 'leader' is one of the few words in the whole world that cannot be bestowed by the stroke of a pen. You can be made a supervisor, manager, CEO, senator, president by the stroke of a pen, but you can't be made a leader; that has to be earned every day."

Every now and then, Charlotte would unconsciously hold her gold sand dollar and look off into space deep in thought.

"I had the opportunity of working with a lot of different organizations over the years. I saw something again and again that bothered me tremendously. In every organization there are some people who think, as they rise on the organizational chart, that somewhere along the way this

term 'leader' just automatically attaches itself to
their name. It does not. Your position on the organizational chart at Owen Industrial only gives
you one thing—your position on the organizational chart. It will never, ever make you a leader."

She stood up, reached deep into her coveralls
and took out a really nice pencil. "Do you know
what this is?"

"It's a pencil."

I was relieved to finally get a question I could
answer.

"Do you know the history of pencils?"

One out of two ain't bad. "No, I don't."

"Pencils go back to the ancient Egyptians and
Romans. People still say lead pencils, but there's
no lead in them anymore. It's graphite. Kind of
interesting how they are made. The plain old
wooden pencil that every school child uses goes
back to the late 1700's, invented by some French-
man."

Charlotte smiled as she admiringly twirled the
teal and white pencil in her hand.

"This is one of the things that we take for granted
because they are everywhere, except when you
need one. This one is mechanical. It's new." And
with a big laugh, she said, "Probably only goes
back 100 years. This is one of the great tools of
the world when you think about it. In association
with its first cousin, the ink pen, it has written all
the great books, the *Bible*, *Declaration of Inde-
pendence*, *Gettysburg Address*, and signed peace

treaties to keep the world safe. It enabled Einstein, Pasteur, Dickinson, Eli Whitney, and the Wright Brothers to capture their thoughts and move on. It has helped find the cure for just about every disease known to man.

"This little tool right here will enable you to follow through on every commitment you make for the rest of your life. You will never forget anything, ever. Get a little notebook, something that will fit in your pocket, and take it with you everywhere you go. Record everything—every commitment, every appointment, and your 'do' list."

"You mean I should have it with me literally all of the time, day and night?" I asked.

"Well, there is one time when you don't have to have it with you," she said with a devilish grin.

I felt I had to take up for myself.

"I do have a computer on my desk and a desk top calendar."

"Those are great, but what happens when you walk five feet away from your desk? Jake, you make commitments everywhere you go: down the hall, up on the second floor, out on the shop floor, in the cafeteria, riding in the car, at home, too. There has been nothing invented to this point that can completely replace the simple pencil."

She took a sip of juice and looked out toward the street. One of her neighbors was walking toward the house.

"Uh, oh, stand by, here comes Gladys Cran-

Courage to Lead

ford. She has seen you here a couple of times and wants to check you out. I want you to take this pencil and use it."

"Oh, I can't do that. It's a beautiful pencil, must have been a gift."

"It was, but I've got a whole box of these. When I took over the company, and it became apparent I wasn't going to bankrupt the place, thanks to all my great people, I became somewhat of a novelty in the business community. The women's movement is what they called it, and I lucked out because I hit it just right. Not many women were running things, so I got asked to speak to just about every service organization within 100 miles. I hit them all in Callaway, too. It was terrific, and I talked to mostly men. I had this little speech about leadership. I gave the same one every time, and they loved it."

She was on a roll now. I could tell she was proud of this, and I could just see her up there ranting and raving like she did to me and mesmerizing her audience.

"I've got to hurry, here comes Gladys. Anyway, just about every single organization gave me a pen and pencil set. I had an acceptance speech that went something like, 'Oh, what a beautiful gift. I've never seen one quite like it. I know I'll enjoy this for a long time.' I got so many, I gave them away as Christmas presents until I gave one to my good friend, Bill Fuller. He had given it to me the year before when he was president of the local Rotary. I really messed up on that one. So here, I've got a dozen more just like it."

"Thank you so much."

Gladys Cranford approached the porch. She was about the same age as Charlotte, dressed casually in a corduroy shirt and blue jeans.

"Good morning, Charlotte."

"Good morning, Gladys. Jake, this is my good friend, Gladys Cranford. Gladys, this is Jake Howe, my new boyfriend. He's from Callaway."

"In your dreams," Gladys said with a sideways glance toward me. "Nice to meet you, Jake. Charlotte, you know we have our first meeting of the year of the Garden Club next Thursday at twelve o'clock at the Rec Center. I wanted to make sure you got the word. The rumor is that you will be nominated for president, so don't be late and bring a sandwich with you."

Charlotte threw out her thumb like a hitchhiker and pointed toward the rear of the house. With just a hint of sarcasm, she said, "Well, if the club could see the rose bushes in the back yard that have died from neglect, I am sure you would reconsider."

Gladys laughed and turned to walk away.

"Got to run and catch Margaret before her hair appointment," she hollered over her shoulder. She winked as she stopped to "check me out" one last time.

"You're too cute for Charlotte, and I'm available for lunch," she joked.

Courage to Lead

As I blushed, they both just howled, and I had a sobering thought.

Wouldn't it be something if Charlotte got these women organized on a really important issue? How would you like to be on the opposing side of Charlotte McArthur leading 16 hostile and passionate women, ages 60 to 70? Just the thought of it made me nervous.

It was time to go. She looked drained. These discussions brought back tremendous memories, and she did get emotional. It was easy to see that her initial fear of the business world became her second love, a close second to her children.

As I got up to leave, she took a small beat-up, leather-covered book from her coveralls and asked if she could borrow the pencil back for a second. She turned to Thursday and wrote "Garden Club, 12:00 noon, Rec Center, take sandwich."

She gave the pencil back and said, "Thanks. Have a great week."

Eight

*I*t wasn't a great week, but it was better and as Charlotte said, "Success is progress toward your goal, not necessarily reaching the goal." If that's true, then I was encouraged. I got out a little notebook a supplier had given me about six months before, that I immediately had thrown into a drawer. Lucky, I usually throw them away. However, it was working. I did not forget a single meeting, and I was religiously writing down commitments. It was astounding how many I made in a week and scary to think how many I must have failed to follow through on in the past. She was right; we are not smart enough to efficiently organize our lives in our heads.

I got all my supervisors a book and showed them how to use it. It immediately boosted our productivity. I also found that it freed up my mind to do what I was paid to do, manage and lead. Instead of spending time trying to remember meetings and commitments, I started spending time thinking about the big picture and visualizing how we could do better.

Charlotte said leaders spend a lot of time with their people just listening and walking around. I started having coffee in the cafeteria every morning from about 7:45 to 8:15. I spoke to every person coming off third shift and coming on first. They all passed through the cafeteria, and I could tell they appreciated the personal contact. I learned things about them and their families I filed away for future reference.

One thing I did forget was to ask Charlotte about the one ingredient that is critical for success as a leader. I wrote that down for next Saturday.

After dinner on Thursday night, Susan went to see a friend whose mom was sick. I got the kids into bed and had just settled into my chair with the paper when she returned.

"How's Becky's mom?" I inquired.

"She's gonna make it. The doctors were concerned at first, but it looks like she's turned the corner."

Susan sat down in her chair. Her body language suggested she really didn't care to talk. I continued to read as she stared into nowhere.

"Tell me about Charlotte," she finally said. Her tone was almost one of jealousy. It was as if the real question was why I was spending so much time with Charlotte and sharing things with her that I would not share with my wife.

"Charlotte is an unusual person who has had a very difficult life. She is absolutely uncompromising on some things, but is flexible on most and a great listener."

"What do you talk about?"

"About 99% of our conversation has been about business and leadership. She enjoys her Garden Club, but it's easy to see she misses the rough and tumble challenge of the business world."

"I'm sure she enjoys your company."

"I think she does, but I know I'm getting the better end of the deal. I'm getting my master's degree on Saturday morning from a world class expert . . . for free."

"Does she have many close friends?"

"Not that I can tell. She spent all of her time with a demanding business and her children, and some of the extras we take for granted, like close friends and hobbies, were a casualty of her efforts."

"Is she happy?"

"It's hard to tell. She's not the kind of person

who would ever let you know. With her husband gone, kids half way across the country, and the business sold, I can't imagine her being truly fulfilled."

"How old are her children?"

"A little younger than us I guess. Charlotte says they are doing well. One is a patent lawyer, single, and the other is married with a family. Neither one lives in Eagle Springs, which disappoints her."

Susan's tone softened, sensing this woman shared some of her same values, especially where family was concerned.

"That's a real tribute to her dedication as a single parent," Susan said, with a hint of admiration. "I have always thought that the one person in the world who deserves the most credit is the single mom or dad who works and also does a great job with the children."

"Susan, sometimes I feel that you're a single parent, and I do appreciate what you do for the kids. I just hope in the near future I can get my mind off the problems at work and help out more here."

"I hope so, too," she concluded.

That statement was about as close as she ever got to saying what was obvious to us both. Our relationship had suffered because of my work, and the responsibility was totally mine to make it right.

"Why don't you go with me this Saturday? She would love to meet you."

"I think I'll wait," Susan said. "It sounds like you're making real progress, and I wouldn't want to interfere. There's plenty of time to meet her later."

I was making progress. I was starting to feel comfortable with her. It had never been easy for me to expose my shortcomings and fears, but somehow my admiration and respect for her overcame my fear and vulnerability. I hated to think our meetings would end some day.

This particular Saturday was a nasty one. The clouds were getting ready to dump some much-needed rain. The old guys in Wagner were drinking their coffee and waving, but they also had moved closer to the front door of the cafe. Just as I pulled up to Charlotte's house, it started to sprinkle. Charlotte yelled, "Better hurry! This is gonna be a big one."

I reached the porch just as it started to pour. It smelled great. The concrete driveway was steaming, and I knew the grass and plants were happy. Charlotte said, "Come inside. When the wind comes up, we'll get drenched."

Her home was just as I expected. It was a reflection of her personality: everything in its place, clean and neat, pictures of her family everywhere. It was also comfortable and warm, not like some homes where I hesitate to sit down for fear of messing up the pillows. Or, God forbid, I ever spill something and give someone cardiac arrest on the spot. Her home made me feel as if I could take my shoes off, put up my feet and just relax. The only visible testament to her success was a small plaque on the wall proclaiming her "Eagle Springs Mother of the Year."

Graciously, she led me to a big chair.

"Sit here. It was my husband's, and the unwritten rule was that no one but Wilson could sit here. To this day, our children still won't sit in it, something about the ghost of Dad coming back to haunt 'em."

She chuckled.

"He only had this about a year before he died and since nobody sits in it, it's practically brand new. I sit in it every once in awhile just to test the ghost theory, but it's too big for me. How do you like it?"

"It's terrific."

And it was, solid leather with an ottoman to match. It wrapped around me like a favorite quilt. It was the kind of gift you give yourself for doing something significant.

"He had it specially made for himself," she explained proudly, "when he sold a patent on a manufacturing process."

On the mantelpiece above the stone fireplace was a small anvil about six inches high. "What's the story behind the anvil?" I asked.

"My husband's grandfather was a blacksmith. He told Wilson that when a blacksmith molds a horseshoe, he heats and then he beats it. When he does this, the horseshoe gets tougher.

"He gave the anvil to Wilson when he started the business, and told him when he had setbacks and disappointments to look at the anvil and say 'I'm getting tougher.' In the early days Wilson had many conversations with that anvil . . . I have too.

"One of the many things Wilson passed on to me was that leaders look upon setbacks as learning experiences. Accept the fact you will have disappointments, and use them as learning blocks on the long journey of becoming a leader."

By the chair on a glass top table was a picture of Charlotte and her girls when they were small. There was a note on the frame that said, *Instructions For Use: Pick up, look at the picture and say, "My, what beautiful women!"* I usually do as instructed, so I said, "My, what beautiful women!"

Charlotte grinned.

"I gave that to Wilson a long time ago. He worked so hard that sometimes he forgot what was going on around here, so I had to remind him. Jake, don't ever forget about what is going on at home. It's important, and your family needs to be appreciated, too. The principles of leadership we have been discussing should be applied at home as well as work."

I knew she was right.

"Your home is beautiful," I remarked.

"Thank you. We had a lot of good times here and a few sad ones, but it's home. About the time

I could afford a bigger house the kids were leaving, and I didn't need it. That's the way it usually works, right? How about some coffee? How do you like it?"

"Black, so it will kickstart my heart."

"So tell me about your home growing up," she said.

"Nothing special, really."

And it wasn't. I remember going to friends' homes like this, wishing I could have something similar. I learned early on the difference between a house and a home.

"You mentioned your dad. Did he remarry?"

"No, he never did. He had some lady friends along the way, but nothing serious. I guess after Mom passed away, he was so busy with me it just never worked out."

"I sure can understand that. Did you two get along?"

"Not really. He was hard-working, honest and incredibly smart. But he was also moody and not a particularly happy person. We sort of drifted apart as I got older. That is something I really miss, not knowing my mom or dad. I guess that is one of the things I am struggling with now, to make sure the same thing doesn't happen to my family."

"Did he ever talk about your mom?"

"Occasionally. Sort of strange when I think about it, but he never did talk much about her. I do remember one Christmas when I was about 10, he said he wished my mom could be there. I always wondered about my mom, what she was like. I don't even have a picture of her."

"Where is your dad now?"

"I don't know. The last time I heard anything he had moved to south Florida and was in poor health. He loved the ocean and fishing, so it makes sense he would end up there, probably down in the Keys somewhere. He used to go there on vacation. His sister, my Aunt Sally, used to keep me informed, but she died about a year ago so I have lost touch."

"You mean nobody knows where he is?"

"Yes, he wanted it that way. He became sort of a recluse. Aunt Sally said after my mom died, he really changed. He knows where I am if he needs me, but he has never gotten in touch, and I don't expect he ever will. I don't know a single soul who knows where he is."

Charlotte's eyes glazed over. I avoided eye contact until she could regain her composure. Being the strong family person she is, it was easy to see how she could be affected by my story. I just know when people care about me, and it was obvious that her intentions and actions toward me were perfectly matched up.

I had never shared my story with anyone except Susan, and it felt good to get it off my chest. I had been carrying that baggage around for a long time, and it seemed I had just lightened the load a little. It was good to feel I could trust her, and I did.

Charlie Farrell

Maybe it was the talk about families, or maybe she wasn't feeling well—she still had a nagging little cough that I had noticed the week before—but our meeting that day wasn't like the others. It may have been the most fruitful, but for different reasons. I didn't forget to ask the question I'd written down, but for some reason, I thought this just wasn't the right time. It could wait.

She walked me to the door, hugged me gently around the neck and said goodbye.

Nine

The next week was good. I was starting to enjoy work a little more. Even Susan mentioned that my morale had improved. The concepts Charlotte talked about were so simple. It was really common sense, but the problem was, as she said so succinctly, "Common sense is an uncommon thing."

She also made a point that leaders understand the difference between being efficient and being effective.

She told a story about a friend of hers who

Charlie Farrell

bought a two story house in Eagle Springs. The upstairs bathroom floor was cracked and had to be replaced. Her friend was riding by the house one day, so she stopped in. She met the man who had just finished the tile work and said, "It looks great. The tile is beautiful, but it is the *upstairs* bathroom floor that needs to be replaced." He could have been the best tile man in America, the very finest craftsman, but how much was his work worth at that moment? Zero. In fact, less than zero because he had to replace, at his own expense, what he had done and then do the right job.

That's the difference. Efficient is doing things right, while effective is doing the right things. You have to be both, but leaders always think in terms of being effective first. Am I doing the right things in my personal life as well as in my business life?

The next Saturday I couldn't go to Eagle Springs because of my youngest child's birthday party. I called Charlotte to let her know. She sounded cheerful and said if it worked out the following Saturday, to come on down; she'd be right there.

Whoever came up with the idea of bringing ponies to your home for the kids to ride ought to be shot. It took me a week to get the mess cleaned up, but the kids had fun. The benefit outweighed the cost this time, especially since nobody fell off and broke an arm.

Watching the kids made me think back to my conversation with Mike Patton. There were two

Courage to Lead

kids at the party, not mine, who seemed to monopolize the other kids' attention. Whatever they wanted to do, the others just naturally seemed to follow. They argued a little about things, but there was no doubt who the leaders were.

The big question remains. Are leaders born or made?

I'd sat through hours of seminars and giant debates whether leadership is innate or learned, and I was never able to answer the question to my satisfaction. It would be interesting to track those two kids for 30 years and see what happens.

But the party brought back a sad memory, too. On my third or fourth birthday, I can't remember which, my parents took me and a few friends to one of those little carnivals that ride the circuit. They had some ponies you could ride for a quarter, and it was the first time I had ever been on a pony.

This day at the carnival was up to that point the most exciting event of my life. I remember the brightly-painted clowns, the popcorn, the crisp autumn night, my first candy apple. I remember clutching the reins with sticky fingers and the teddy bear we almost won. But most of all I remember my mother's laugh.

It is also the last memory I have of my mom.

The next week went well except for two events. One was a run-in with my boss over production. Our human error rate was falling, a positive sign,

Charlie Farrell

but the machine error rate was rising. I had been told by our operators for months that we needed to overhaul machines #3 and #4 and replace #6 altogether. I had put in the requisitions twice, and they were shot down both times.

On Friday my boss, George Thompson, came into my office to discuss the situation. He didn't say it, but I knew someone up the line had brought it to his attention, because proactive was not in his vocabulary, only reactive. He was simply a conduit of good and bad news from the corner office. On his wall calendar he was counting the days to retirement, about 1,050. He had a party planned when the number reached triple digits.

Breathing heavily and perspiring after the "long walk" from his office, George had a habit of plopping down on my work table, wrinkling the paperwork.

"You have got to get this error rate under control. I'm catching hell from the head shed, so what's your plan?" he demanded in his usual loud and pompous manner with some hostility sprinkled in.

I showed him documentation about the falling human error rate, but rising machine errors. I also showed him the requisitions for major overhaul and capital investment with his signature declining the requests.

"We can't spend any money right now," he grunted.

"Fine. I understand that, but my people are

busting their butts down here to do a good job, and they're frustrated as hell because these machines are killing 'em. They can't even leave to go to the bathroom because they're afraid the tolerances will slip. They have to practically live with the machines, not to mention the fact you haven't replaced three people, so now we have one person trying to watch two machines. You're asking me to turn out Picassos with buckets of mud, and it's not working, so what do you want me to do?"

George just shrugged his shoulders. He was good at that when he didn't have the answers, which was most of the time.

"Why don't I take it up with the plant manager?" I snapped.

"The book says that after you have talked with me," he barked sarcastically, "you can take it on up. So you can talk to him if you want to. You have that right, but I strongly suggest you don't rock the boat too hard, if you know what I mean."

My disrespect for him as a person and manager was taking charge. My blood pressure was rising as I heatedly exclaimed, "This boat's got a hole in it and is taking on water. Are we just going to stand around and cheer while it sinks?"

"I wouldn't do it if I were you," George warned as he stormed out, slamming my door behind him.

I was never good at foreign languages, but I knew immediately how to translate that remark: *I've only got 1,050 days to go with a party planned at 999. Just let me get out of here with my re-*

tirement, and I don't give a damn what happens. The boat can settle next to the Titanic, and I'll be down on the farm with a mint julep and a smile—and it wouldn't be in Jake Howe's best interest to upset the plan.

On my way home I was bothered that my people problems didn't end with George. The other challenge is ongoing and its name is Randolph Eugene Lockhart, Jr., nicknamed Skeeter. What a piece of work this guy is. The word to accurately describe this man is not in _Funk & Wagnalls_. The closest thing would be weird-squared. He has it down to a science.

He lives out in the boondocks alone with four blue tick hounds and still drives a twenty-year-old lavender, weathered van which he parks in the farthest corner of the parking lot. Skeeter saunters through the gate with his badge on backwards to aggravate the security guards. Once inside, he throws his lunch into the locker with his leather thongs and beret, leaves the locker door open, and proceeds to the coffee machine. He gets one cup with sugar only, a package of cheese crackers (he calls it his "breakfast of champions"), yells an obscenity to production control, and walks to the time clock. He punches in exactly one second before 8:00 a.m.

Skeeter does all this without the benefit of a watch. His was ripped off his arm two months ago by a machine without the safety guard up, not to mention that wearing watches on the production

Courage to Lead

floor is absolutely forbidden. His clothes range from early Quaker to the hardest rock imaginable. His views on everything are either extreme right or extreme left—it probably depends on the zodiac sign for the day, and he absolutely will not work overtime even if his life depended on it. Nobody knows what he does with his time after work or on weekends, and nobody is about to ask. He makes "Hogan's goat" look like a precision instrument.

His only saving grace is that he is a mechanical genius. Skeeter knows everything about machinery and computers and how they interface. He knows it down to the molecular structure of things. He programmed Hannibal to say to the plant manager, "Mr. Lockhart is your best employee. Give him a raise." The plant manager was not amused.

Skeeter can't explain how he knows these things, but he knows. Any time people have a technical problem, they go to him. He will tell them the solution if he likes them.

He hasn't done anything to get himself fired, although the watch incident came close. He walks a real fine line. I don't like his attitude, and the bottom line is I'd like to see him go.

Taking George and Skeeter home every night was bad enough, but especially difficult on weekends when I should have had my mind on family, having fun and recharging my battery.

The tradition at home on Friday night was

chicken and hot dogs on the grill, a glass of wine and games with the kids until their bedtime. When it was Susan's turn to tuck the kids in, there was a 50/50 chance I would be asleep in my chair by the time she got back to the den.

There was no sleeping in the chair on this Friday night because I had some real heavy things on my mind, specifically the upcoming meeting with the plant manager Monday morning. I was sailing into some pretty treacherous waters with a faulty compass, and, to say the least, I was uneasy.

Susan came in and sat down, flipped off the TV and picked up her book.

"How are you coming with your book?"

"Pretty good. Interesting true story about a family who got tired of the big city rat race, chucked everything and moved to a small town called Ketchikan, Alaska. The husband had flown all his life, so he bought a seaplane and contracted with the logging camps to ferry people and supplies. His wife ran tours for people off the cruise ships. Rugged place, Alaska, but sounds pretty with the glaciers, whales and eagles."

"Yeah, sometimes I feel like chuckin' it, too. If it turns out he's successful, let's call him and see if he needs a helper. I'll load airplanes, and you can work in a salmon factory."

Susan laughed.

"How about let's switch—you work in the salmon factory. You know I don't even like to eat fish, much less clean 'em."

"That's a deal."

My wife knew me too well. She lowered the book, took her glasses off, and in a very direct manner asked, "What's wrong?"

"What would you think if I lost my job?"

It got so quiet the ticking on the wall clock sounded like Big Ben. She just looked at me, trying to process the bomb I had just dropped. Susan was big on security issues. She didn't care so much about a big house or fancy car, but she wasn't much of a risk-taker. The thought of being without a job and all the benefits that go along with big corporate employment made her real nervous. If she had ever written a script for her life, it would read: "Get married, two kids, comfortable house, husband employed by the same company for 40 years, retire together, die together."

After a long pause, she said, "I guess my feelings about it would depend a great deal on why. If you were fired because you had done something wrong or you were not doing your job, I would be very upset. If the reasons are out of your control, that would be different. What's going on?"

I explained to her all that was going on with the work: the rejects, the run-in with my boss, the sorry equipment. I had always separated work from home and had never shared much, but lately it had been very difficult to do that. Susan could sense there were some big issues brewing.

I fully expected her to say, "Well, why don't

you just rock on a little longer and see what happens. Maybe things will change. And by the way, be careful what you say and how you say it on Monday morning."

I was surprised when she said, "It sounds to me as if your thinking is correct. I believe you ought to go in Monday morning, guns blazing, and see how they react. The worst thing that can happen is not all that bad. The most important thing is that you be happy with your work. It's obvious that although you've been happier lately, it is still not what it should be." She concluded, "Be professional and be prepared, but tell it like it is."

Susan closed her book and got into her slippers. Confidently, I said, "I have rehearsed this thing in my mind a hundred times, and I've already practiced once on George Thompson. I'll be prepared, and I do appreciate your support."

She got up, kissed me on the cheek and said, "I know you have a lot of thinking to do, so I'll head on to bed. Come on when you're ready." And with a smile, she whispered, "Be quiet when you leave in the morning and give Charlotte my regards."

In school I had read a lot of Shakespeare. I didn't appreciate until then his insight about "sleep knitting up the raveled sleeve of care." I looked forward each day to this time of respite. I only hoped events would not soon rob me of this one oasis from the anguish, doubt, and frustration.

EAGLE SPRINGS
GARDEN CLUB PARK

Ten

The drive to Eagle Springs was a quick one, as all trips are when I have a lot on my mind. It was as though I had a split personality. One minute I was euphoric over the headway we were making in my department, and the next I was really depressed about the big picture.

I also had a great feeling about the progress I was making as a leader. I may be fooling myself, but I can feel the difference in some people's attitudes. Charlotte said you can't go on "feel"; you have to have objective proof: "indisputable facts," she calls it. The declining human error rate is the only fact I have. However, I can't completely ignore some of the intangibles, and I know they are there.

It had been two weeks since my last visit, and I was excited, tempered somewhat by the upcoming meeting with the plant manager. The old boys in Wagner were still doing their thing and waved a big hello. I'm going to stop in there some day and introduce myself. I feel like I know 'em.

As I pulled in the driveway, Charlotte waved and walked down the steps toward the car. She was dressed in a blue denim shirt, khaki pants, tennis shoes, and the ever-present gold sand dollar.

In her usual cheerful voice, she said, "Let's go for a walk. The coffee is perking and will be ready when we get back. The flowers are blooming, and I'll give you the 50-cent neighborhood tour.

"I'll also have you know that since I saw you last, I was elected president of the Eagle Springs Garden Club. I'll show you some of our handiwork."

"Congratulations, I'm proud to know someone so important."

"Well, it was a close vote between Henrietta Morgan and me. But my speech on the care and feeding of 'blue afghanistanbluedandrums' won the day and it was a proud moment, indeed. Anyway," as she threw her head back and chin up, "that's my story, and I'm sticking with it!"

In her very best mock-serious tone, she concluded, "Another thing about leaders: don't ever let the truth stand in the way of a good story!"

Then she let out one of those "ain't life grand" laughs and said, "Tell me about your week."

I gave her the lowdown on the week with emphasis on my upcoming meeting with the plant manager, and my "good friend," Skeeter Lockhart. As usual, she listened with no comment.

We headed out. It was a beautiful morning. The neighborhood was just what I had expected. All the homes were modest but nice. The lawns and flowers were mature and well tended. These people took pride in what they had and worked hard to maintain it.

I also knew this woman could afford to live anywhere she wanted, but she was comfortable here. These were her kind of people. She knew them all, and they had shared a lot of happiness and sorrow over the years. She had seen their kids grow up and leave and had been to all the weddings and funerals. If ever someone valued substance over form, she did.

She pointed to the white brick house next door.

"John Blackman lives there. He is a retired industrial psychologist. Generally speaking, shrinks make me nervous, but he's a great person and smart as a whip. His hobby is yardwork. See my tool shed over there? On weekends when he came out to work, I could see him from my kitchen. When he disappeared behind my tool shed, I would take off my apron real quick, run out to my shed and grab a rake. Then I'd walk slowly around the side and say, 'Oh, good morning, John, I didn't see you.'

"I would rope him into conversations, which just by coincidence led into the latest people problem I was working on. I got a four-year psychology degree over the back fence. He caught on real quick to all this and sent me a bill one day for $10,000, referencing 'Saturday morning consultations.'

"One day I was really down because I thought nobody appreciated me and all of my hard work. Jake, whether it's a two-person organization or a two-thousand-person organization, it's sometimes lonely, and self-doubt creeps in. John said something that was a big help: 'Virtue is its own reward. If you do right as a leader and are honest and fair, then it really doesn't matter what other people think.' Sometimes that's all the pat on the back you'll get, but sometimes that's all you need.

"About your meeting on Monday—and I can tell you are concerned about it—apply the same principle: be honest and fair, and do your best. If the big boys don't appreciate that, it might be time to look elsewhere. Your reward will be that whatever happens, you'll know that you did the right thing."

"I appreciate your saying that, Charlotte. I have been thinking a lot lately about the meeting—and the consequences."

Courage to Lead

We continued our walk, and we stopped periodically to chat with the neighbors. They were nice people, relaxed, genuine, no pretense. These people had worked hard all of their lives and deserved the serenity and comfort they now enjoyed.

"Charlotte, these people remind me of my Uncle James. When he retired, we asked him what he was going to do. He said, "Nothing, and I won't start until 10:00."

She laughed, and we continued walking.

"Vanessa Cleveland lives there," Charlotte said as she pointed to a white brick house with a gray cupola. "Sad thing. Her husband, Kevin, died in his mid-fifties from a heart attack. He was a mid-level executive for a big printing company and was the hardest working man I've ever seen—literally worked himself to death. He was on medication for high blood pressure and died on the production floor after about his tenth straight 12-hour day.

"At the funeral, the plant manager came up to Vanessa and said he was sorry and that he didn't know Kevin was having problems. I felt like punching him in the mouth. It was his job to know. That's part of being a leader, Jake, knowing how your people are doing, how many hours they are putting in, about their health. Sometimes you have to protect them from themselves.

"Like your superstar, Bill Markston. People like him will never quit. You have to make sure they get time off, take their vacations and that you don't unknowingly take advantage of them."

"You're right. I guess it's easy to lean on the dependable people without considering the toll it takes."

"Speaking of health," Charlotte said, "what do you do to stay in shape?"

"I appreciate your kindness implying that I am in shape, but I'll have to admit I've put on a few extra pounds lately—wish I could blame it on your coffee cake, but I can't. It's just that I have been so preoccupied with things at work that exercise has been put on the back burner."

She became serious.

"Jake, my husband put exercise on the back burner, and it cost us dearly. You're not doing anybody any favors by disregarding your health. It's really more important than family because if you don't have your health you might end up without your family and them without you."

This was the only time I ever sensed she was disappointed in her husband. Under the circumstances I could understand why. Then I thought about my children and a minister coming to the door . . .

She looked directly at me.

"Jake, you can't lead very well from a hospital bed. Commit to me that you will make your health a high priority."

"I promise I will."

And I meant it.

Courage to Lead

"You mentioned all the problems at work seem to end up on your desk," she said as we continued walking.

"Yes."

"That's a common occurrence," she said, as she took out her little notebook and a mechanical pencil. She grinned. "Told you I had a bunch of these."

We stopped walking, and I watched her write a few sentences. She tore the page out, handed it to me like a doctor's prescription, and said, "Put this memo out Monday morning, and you'll take care of 90% of your problems."

> FROM: Jake Howe
> TO: Production Department
> SUBJECT: Problems
> As of 9:00 a.m. today I will no longer accept a problem without a suggested solution.

We came to the Eagle Springs Garden Club Park. It was impressive. I don't know a waxed myrtle from a petunia, but the colors—lavenders, whites, reds, blues, and pinks—were beautiful. And the fragrances reminded me of walking past a perfume counter in a department store—just incredible!

"This land is owned by Russell Millford, who lives right there in the gray house. He's tried to sell the land from time to time, but for some

Charlie Farrell

unexplained reason," as she grinned mischievously, "the *For Sale* signs keep disappearing.

"One day Henrietta Morgan, whom I so soundly whipped for the president's position, was here working when a prospect came by to look over the property. This fellow asked Henrietta if she knew anything about the property. She held up a dead flower and told him it used to be a nuclear waste disposal site. He left rather quickly and never returned. Old Russell knows he's got a good deal— sixteen crazy women tilling his soil for free. He's got tons of money anyway."

"Remind me to avoid all business transactions with you Garden Club types," I said. "You folks are emotionally attached to this dirt, and that makes you dangerous."

"You betcha," she said with a proud smile.

We walked through the park, and she pointed out all the different flowers, plants and trees: holly, junipers, lugustrums, sycamore, barberry, jasmine and maple. I didn't know one from the other, but I nodded my head as if I understood a little bit. She knew better.

As she broke a dead branch off a crepe myrtle, she continued. "I like gardening because it's such a challenge. It's the plant and me against the elements. You take a small plant—nurture it, feed it, sometimes train it—it will grow and prosper. If you do a good job, one day it can survive on its own. That tree over there, the maple. I planted that tree 10 years ago when it was only a foot high. Look at it now. I haven't had to do a thing to it in years; it's surviving on its own."

I looked at the beautiful tree and thought about the time she had invested caring for it at the beginning.

"Leadership is like that. You take people, some of them young. If you feed, nurture and train them, after awhile they can pretty much function on their own.

"Plants are like people in another way. They're all different, but they all have a purpose, a very specific purpose in the big scheme of things. These azaleas give color and are enjoyable to look at. That tree provides food in the form of fruit. Those big maples have several purposes. They form a barrier against the noise, wind and the sight of a busy street. They also provide shade for these hostas and snow trilliums to produce flowers, because they can't be in the direct sun all day. These junipers provide ground cover and keep the grass down.

"A beautiful garden like this requires a lot of planning—putting the right plants in the right places. If you were to let the ivy get too close to the gardenias, in a very short time the ivy would overrun them.

"Same with business. You have to have the right people in the right place, and not based just on technical competence."

"I always thought synergy meant two people working together could always accomplish more than if they worked independently," I said.

"Well, that's great in theory, but it's just not always true in the real world. A lot depends on their personalities. Some people just naturally work well together, and some people don't."

She reached down and pulled a weed.

"I learned that the hard way. We had a problem one time . . . let me rephrase that. We had some sort of problem all the time, which is another lesson you seem to be learning. There are problems all the time, it's just a matter of which one you're going to deal with next. But that's the job of a leader, either preventing problems from happening or fixing them when they occur.

"Anyway, we had a production problem, so I picked the four smartest people we had, and we had some smart ones, to solve it. It was a disaster. They never came up with the answer; they argued and friendships were lost. It was awful. The problem was me, and I wasn't even on the team. My four brightest people were what I called Bengal Tigers—hard headed, egotistical, proud, not good with people or details, impatient, all wanted to be in charge. I had built a team based on technical competence and IQ, and it didn't work."

"So what did you do?"

"I talked with John Blackman. He said you have to build teams based on behavioral style and personality, not just technical competence. He said it's necessary to have a Bengal Tiger, someone who'll take charge and ram it through. But you also need people who are good with details and some who value the team approach and are loyal. It's critical to have someone who'll monitor the bottom line, and someone else who can sell the ideas to the decision-makers. We all have strengths and weaknesses, so we need to surround ourselves with people who are good at the things we are not. I disbanded the team the next day, rebuilt it, and the new team solved the problem in a month."

She looked up at some high-flying geese in perfect formation. "Someday, if we have time, I'll have to tell you about geese and leadership. There are some interesting parallels." I was beginning to wonder if there was anything this self-educated woman didn't know something about.

She had gotten so wrapped up in her plants and geese, it seemed that she had forgotten about Skeeter Lockhart. But that was okay; she was having fun.

I shouldn't have been surprised when she said, "Now this little plant right here is your Skeeter. Look at those thorns. Get close to that fella, and he'll hurt you. The other plants don't like him, and they won't get close to him either. However, this plant is critical to the process. It brings a talent, if you will, that these other plants don't have. They accept this plant the way it is, not the way they want it to be.

"That's what you must do with Skeeter; accept him the way he is, not as you want him to be. When you described him to me, you talked for 10 minutes about superfluous things: the way he dresses, the truck he drives, the coffee he drinks, his religious and political views, his locker. And you talked about his incredible skill and talent for only 10 seconds. Do the others like him?"

"Well, kind of."

"Does he cause a problem?"

"Other than the watch incident, no."

"Have you ever worn a ring or watch on the production floor?" (There's another one of those questions.)

I was silent because I knew she had me.

"Does he do the job as required in the job description?"

"Yes."

"With his incredible knowledge, he probably goes above and beyond because he doesn't have to tell anybody anything," she asserted.

Charlotte sat down on a concrete bench and eyed some beautiful cardinals in a bird bath.

"One other way people are like plants is that some, like that maple tree, can survive on their own after a while. Others need constant care and attention or they will perish. Same with people— most need ongoing attention, some more than others, but they all need it. Did Skeeter do anything significant this week?"

I thought back quickly to Wednesday.

"Yes, he helped Patricia McDuffy get our #2 machine back online after a power outage."

"Did you tell him thank you?"

"No, I didn't," I sheepishly had to admit.

"Jake, I want to challenge you that sometime on Monday you go to Skeeter and say thanks. Not in a general way, but very specifically for his help on #2.

"Jake, do you remember that old saying, 'sticks and stones will break my bones, but words will never hurt me?'"

"Sure, I said that a thousand times as a kid."

"Well, that saying is not true. The wounds from sticks and stones will heal someday, but the wounds from the wrong words, or the lack of words, sometimes never heal and can last a lifetime.

"There's a good chance Skeeter grew up in a situation where there were only wrong words, or the lack of words, and he may be searching, in his own strange way, for someone to fill that void.

"Skeeter is not bad; he's just different. Leaders have to learn to work with all kinds, and you've got all kinds in a big company: young, old, men, women, blacks, whites, foreigners, Christians, Jews and atheists.

"If you fired all 50 and hand-picked 50 you like, whom would you hire?"

"I'd probably hire people who share my thoughts and values," I replied.

"Right, you'd hire fifty people just like you. Do you need 50 Jake clones running around on the production floor? No, you don't. You need people who have talents you don't have. People like Skeeter are hard to find. Talent like his doesn't come along very often, and it would be a shame to waste it.

"Leaders have to take risks, and the biggest risk you'll ever take will involve people. And it's not 50/50. You as a leader will have to go more than halfway. You cannot go into a relationship saying the other person has to prove himself. You must go in saying, 'I trust you. I accept you the way you are; let's work together toward a common goal.'

"Sometimes you'll be disappointed. Like our children, our employees are our greatest joy and sometimes our greatest sorrow. Just remember one thing: you'll always be promoted by the people who work for you; the boss just brings you the news."

She brushed an ant gently off her ankle.

"I warn you that you are setting yourself up with Skeeter. You may be disappointed or embarrassed by his response, but that's the risk you take.

"See that pretty hydrangea by the start of the woodswalk? Look right next to it. There's a little scraggly something growing there I never noticed before. That doesn't belong there and, if allowed to stay, will harm the hydrangea. So before we leave, we're gonna jerk it out of the ground and get rid of it.

"The most unpleasant thing you will have to learn about leadership is discovering everyone doesn't fit. You'll have to get rid of some. And the quicker you do it, the less painful it will be.

We can pull that plant out of the ground right now by hand or we can wait five years and bring in a bulldozer. But sooner or later, it has to go."

She looked directly into my eyes and became very serious.

"I suggest you try to work things out with Skeeter. If you do your part as a leader and he doesn't do his, then get rid of him. That is your job.

"Of all the skills necessary to be successful, the ability and willingness for leaders to confront negative situations is one of the most important. The cemetery of failed businesses is inundated with the ghosts of men and women who didn't have the courage to confront."

She got up slowly, put her hands on her hips, arched her back, and said, "Let's head back, I'm worn out. I'll have to delegate the rest of this weed-pulling to my lieutenants."

On the way back she pointed out the home of the Wrenshalls. "Their son, Lewis, worked for me every summer in high school and college. I took him on full time after he graduated, like you, with an engineering degree. Probably not as smart as Skeeter, but close. Great kid. Worked with us about five years and was progressing nicely, but I noticed over a couple of weeks he was distracted and worried about something. So I called him into my office and told him he couldn't leave until he told me what was wrong.

"He knew he'd been had, so he told me he had an incredible offer from a competitor to buy into a good business. He was all upset because of the family relationship and our working together since he was a teenager. He was such a loyal kid."

"So what did you do?"

"I fired him on the spot, of course, so he had to take the offer! It was the chance of a lifetime for him."

"It hurts to lose good people," I said.

"That's another thing about leadership, Jake. You're going to lose some good people along the way. But I measured some of my success by how many job offers my people received. I took it as a supreme compliment that somebody else wanted a leader I helped develop.

"A leader's job is to create an environment where good people don't want to leave. And for the most part, we did that. We lost very few. The ones we did lose were like Lewis, who just had opportunities they couldn't pass up."

As we got closer to her house, I asked her to tell me the story behind the gold sand dollar. As she held it gently between her thumb and forefinger, she was unusually evasive. "It's a long story," she whispered.

In deep thought, she looked up at the rising sun just peeking through some wispy clouds.

Finally she said, "I do believe in luck. There is good luck, and there is bad luck. You can't do much about bad luck—hurricanes, terrible diseases, floods or recessions. But you must take advantage of good luck.

"I also believe that every individual is presented at certain times with good luck. As with Lewis, it could be a job offer. It could be a chance meeting like the one we had. Or it could be seeing something just as you turn on the TV that sparks a thought that enables you to invent something significant. What if you had been delayed by a traffic light that caused you to turn on the TV 30 seconds later, and you missed the spark? That is luck. Leaders not only recognize it, they are willing to take advantage of the opportunity and accept the associated risks."

"Isn't there a connection between luck and hard work?" I asked. "I mean, it doesn't seem fair that sometimes undeserving people have all the luck."

"Occasionally that's true, but there is also no doubt that the harder you work, the luckier you seem to get. The person who goes out into the world, interacts with competent people, studies hard, and looks for opportunities is going to be luckier than the person who stays home waiting for the mailman to deliver the million-dollar lottery check. Sometimes you make your own good luck."

I asked her about the important ingredient for success as a leader she had mentioned in an earlier meeting.

"There are some things you can't be given, that you have to figure out for yourself. I never said I'd give it to you, because I can't. I said there's one ingredient missing. You have to discover it

Charlie Farrell

on your own, and you will. It's not that you can't be a good leader without it, because you can. However, in my opinion, this one factor is the difference between being a good leader and a great leader. I also have a premonition that you're on the threshold of that discovery. Don't think about it; don't worry about it. It will come to you naturally."

We arrived back at the house. The coffee was hot and wonderful, and there was store-bought cheesecake with fresh strawberries on top.

"Sorry I couldn't make the coffee cake this week, but I have been so busy with other things I didn't have the time," she apologized. "I'll try to be a better hostess next time."

As I cut a piece, I said, "I like coffee cake, but I have to admit cheesecake is my favorite. So you did just great."

She winked and said, "Just a lucky guess."

Eleven

On Sunday night, I really started to bear down, preparing myself for the meeting with Robert Ellisor, which would be right after the usual Monday morning managers' meeting.

"Are you ready for tomorrow?" Susan asked.

"I think so."

"What's he like?"

"He's a first class bean counter," I responded. "And not to make a pun, doesn't know beans about manufacturing."

"Does he come around often?"

Charlie Farrell

"He pretty much stays in his office going over the numbers. When he gets out in the plant, it's because he's seen something in the numbers and is trying to see how he can save another nickel."

"What does he look like?" Susan asked. "I've never even met him."

"He's slightly built, about your dad's height, graying hair. Forty-five years old give or take, wears wire-rimmed glasses. His clothes are like his office—immaculate, and he always wears a suit. Doesn't smile much; he kinda looks like your friendly undertaker, which may be prophetic if, as it appears, he was sent here to preside over the demise of Owen Industrial-Callaway Division."

"Is he smart?"

"Maybe too smart. The best description would be introverted intellectual. He was president of the Mensa Society in Chicago, and on his credenza are books on Aristotle, Plato, and the complete unabridged writings of Jean-Paul Sartre, whoever that is."

"Does he ever get mad about things?"

"I have never seen him show any emotion over any issue. And that's one thing I've got to remember tomorrow—don't get emotional. I also need to remember he doesn't appreciate profanity. He's not like George Thompson who will only listen to screaming and hollering."

"What's his management style?"

"Details. When the big one hits, if I see my life flash before my eyes I'm sure I will hear him

Courage to Lead

say, 'Would you do some more study on that, and back it up with some real world numbers.' He will respond positively only if I back up my points with the facts. The word 'feel' drives him bonkers.

"I'll have to give him credit, though. He is prompt, extremely courteous, and follows through to the second on commitments." I didn't fully appreciate that wonderful trait until my little go-around with Charlotte over the Bill Markston vacation incident.

The Monday morning meeting was like all the others: mother duck, Robert Ellisor, with all his little ducklings quacking their approval at every statement, even if we thought differently. His manner and obvious intelligence intimidated most of the managers. I don't really know him any better now than the first day I met him.

He and I have had several disagreements over the previous year, but we both have honored an unspoken rule to always do it in the privacy of his office or mine. All the others, except for Betty Robinson, are content to just quack and waddle along. Betty is definitely a Bengal Tiger.

When his carefully-prepared agenda had been completed exactly on schedule, it was as if the last item said, "Now get up and leave," which is exactly what everybody did. Robert and I walked into his office without a word, and he closed the door. He pointed to a chair next to his desk, sat down and folded his hands on his immaculately clean desk. Calmly, he asked, "Jake, what can I do for you?"

I went through my speech point-by-point. I had prepared charts and graphs and brought copies of denied requisitions. I'm sure Robert was impressed because he never once disputed the numbers. And he never asked the one question which undid most of the others: "Are you absolutely certain?" He knew the numbers better than anyone on earth, and he knew I had done my homework.

After presenting the figures, I asked some of the hard questions we all had: "Is corporate planning to close the plant? Sell the plant? Transfer our work to Kingston? How about the repair and replacement of equipment? Where are the training dollars? Is there a date which I could expect to replace the three people I had lost?" Orders had definitely picked up, and we were really scrambling.

He listened intently, another one of his fine qualities. He sat back in his chair, removed his glasses, and in his calm and deliberate way, began.

"Jake, I appreciate your thoughts, and I especially appreciate your preparation. I'm afraid my response is not going to be all that you want, but I do have a thought.

"First, I don't know the answers to all of your questions, and some of the answers I do know, I'm not at liberty to discuss. All I can tell you is that I was sent here with very specific marching orders, two of which are to cut costs and to find

Courage to Lead

out who the warriors are.

"There are some decisions being made up at corporate, which I am not privy to. It is my understanding that some sort of announcement is imminent. As you know, the word 'imminent' and I don't get along too well, since that could mean five minutes, five days or five months. I'd like to have a hard date for it, but I don't.

"My thought is that Carlton Dallas, corporate vice president of manufacturing will be here tomorrow. You have some valid questions, and I would be more than happy to set you up one-on-one with him."

If leadership is courage, then this was the ultimate: one-on-one with the man they call "Jaws" in what could be an adversarial situation. I was in deep water and had just stepped off a sandbar. Water was one-half inch below my nose with a big wave on the horizon. I also sensed a dorsal fin headed right toward me. But I remembered what Charlotte said about confronting negative situations. I assumed my best low-key professional manner, hoping I wouldn't choke on the words.

"I would like very much to meet with him."

Robert got up, walked toward the door and said, "I'll let you know when. Plan on no more than 15 minutes."

He smiled slightly. I had the feeling he was thinking Carlton would just chew me up and spit me out, thereby eliminating one more of Robert's problems.

"He's different from me," Robert said. "Don't throw too many numbers at him and get to the point quickly. Patience is not in his vocabulary."

Carlton Dallas. I'd met him a few times on plant tours. He walks fast and thinks faster. On each tour he gets out on the floor among the people, talking, slapping them on the back, joking, looking at the equipment, asking questions, congratulating people for longevity, for exceeding production goals, or for having an extra clean work area.

When he gets around to the managers, he asks very specific closed-end questions: "Are you married? What's your wife's name? How many children? How long have you worked here? What was the production rate last month? Expected this month? What is the one thing that would make your job easier? Do you work out? If yes, good. If no, why not?" It's unusual for him to announce he's coming. He believes in walking in the back door literally unannounced because he wants to see things as they really are.

Everyone in the company knows the legend of Carlton Dallas, especially after the last corporate newsletter had a full two-page article on him. He is a Georgia Tech mechanical engineering graduate and All-American football player. The NFL drafted him in the second round, and he played pro football for a year and a half until a linebacker blind-sided him and separated him from the football and his senses.

While he was hospitalized for his concussion, he figured there had to be a better way to make a living. He returned to Georgia Tech and earned his master's degree, but still longing for more excitement, entered the Marine Corps. After Quantico, he volunteered for Ranger School and was made a Force Recon platoon commander stationed in Hawaii.

He was three months away from discharge. It was a Sunday afternoon, and he was on the beach at Kaneohe Bay right across from Chinaman's Hat. He was with his bride of three weeks, having just married his college sweetheart. As they were talking about how life doesn't get any better than this, a military sedan pulled up, and his company commander ran down and hustled him into the car, leaving his wife on the beach. Two hours later, he and his platoon were on a C141 heading west.

He knew it wasn't a game when they handed out live ammunition somewhere over the Pacific.

Some terrorists had bombed our embassy. His platoon was helicoptered into a terrorist camp in the middle of the night with orders to capture the leader. A big fire fight ensued. They captured the leader and three others and killed 10 on the way out. He got all his men in the helicopter, and he was being pulled aboard as the aircraft lifted off. He was shot in the back. The bullet went straight through him, missing his heart by an inch and killing the young Marine who had pulled him aboard.

Dallas was awarded the Silver Star and Purple Heart, and medically discharged on the day he was supposed to get out anyway. He had lived a lifetime, and he was just 26 years old.

Dallas took a job with Owen and has been with them ever since. He was the youngest-ever vice-president of production, youngest-ever plant manager and is the youngest-ever vice president of manufacturing. He is 45 years old on a fast track to the corner office on the 47th floor. Nobody is trying or even pretending to stand in his way. About two more shades of gray and he will be there. He is demanding but fair, smart, bottom-line-oriented, fearless—a real golden boy. He is held in awe by everyone who knows him well, and has the utmost respect from those like me who know him only by reputation. I was scared to death and excited at the same time.

Monday night, surprisingly, I slept well. I had already made the speech twice, although the one to George Thompson didn't really count. I was basically going to give the same pitch to Carlton Dallas I had given to Robert Ellisor without all the numbers.

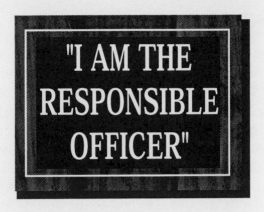

"I AM THE RESPONSIBLE OFFICER"

Twelve

obert Ellisor called, and I was to meet Carlton at 11:00. He, like Charlotte, demanded a first name basis. We were to meet in Robert's office. The door was open when I got there, so I walked in. Carlton got up from behind the desk and met me halfway across the room with a handshake you'd better be ready for.

"Nice to see you again, Jake. How's your family?" Dallas asked cheerfully as he pulled Robert's chair from behind the desk and placed it right in front of where he gestured for me to sit.

Charlie Farrell

"Great, thanks for asking."

He was dressed in a long-sleeve white shirt with a navy blue and burgundy tie, minus the coat. He had closely-cropped dark hair, just beginning to gray. And I had never noticed a slight indentation on the left side of his nose, probably a reminder of his NFL days. He had a thick neck and carried his 200-plus pounds like someone who still values physical fitness.

He picked up some computer printouts from the desk, sat down and got right to the point. "Robert mentioned you had some interesting observations. I'd like to hear them."

I began the presentation which I had rehearsed to about 10 minutes so there would be time at the end. I was not going to go over 15 minutes, except by his invitation.

Every now and then he would hold his hand up for me to stop, and he would look into his computer printouts to verify my numbers. Then he would put his hand down and look at me, and I would continue. Just as I was beginning to wrap up, he interrupted.

"Jake, why is all this important?"

This question I hadn't anticipated. I paused for a second and responded instinctively.

"It's the people. The people here are terrific, and they deserve better than what they've been getting. We have a few renegades, but for the most part, they are loyal and hard-working. Some of them have given their hearts and souls to this

company. Their families depend on it. It's all
they've known. And I have found with just a little
bit of attention, they respond positively, as they
have this past year under very difficult circumstances. With just a little help in a few key areas,
we could really make the company some money
down here."

He abruptly stood up and said, "Is there anything else?"

"The water cooler doesn't work. We get water,
but it's not cold," I blurted. I knew it was a poor
response, but it was the only thing I could think
of at the moment.

"I'll get back to you through Ellisor by noon
tomorrow," Carlton shot back.

He shook my hand and left. I watched him walk
hurriedly toward the front door. Robert Ellisor was
coming in the opposite direction. Without breaking stride, Carlton barked something at Robert and
continued on. Robert Ellisor looked at me and
shrugged his shoulders as if to say, "What was
that all about?"

Some days you eat the bear. Some days the bear
eats you. I headed back to production without the
faintest clue how our meeting had gone.

The route back took me by machine #6, which
had gotten to the point only Skeeter could produce
acceptable results. He was bending over beside
the machine looking at the electronic calibration
equipment. I stopped and said, "Skeeter, I want
to tell you how much I appreciate your helping

Patricia McDuffy last week on machine #2. You did a great job."

Skeeter never stood up. He just turned his head toward me as I started talking, and when I finished, he turned his head back to the equipment without saying a word. I continued walking.

Well, Charlotte can't be right all the time. That was absolutely the biggest waste of a compliment in history, and simply confirmed again my feelings about Skeeter.

The rest of the day was uneventful, which was a positive sign in itself. The troops were doing great, and I was proud of 'em.

At about five after five, Skeeter Lockhart came into my office and said, in a very soft voice, "I appreciate your comments today. It's the first time a manager here has ever said thank you." He gently closed the door and left.

The next morning he was ten minutes early to work.

After the kids went to bed, my wife asked, "Did you dazzle Superman today? It looks like your behind is still intact, so it must not have been too bad."

"I don't know; I really don't. If I had to make a bet, I would probably say it didn't go too well. He asked only one question, and I got up on my soapbox and launched into a dialogue about the people. Maybe he wanted me to talk about profits and the company. When I finished, he got up and left the building. I thought he was supposed to be there most of the day."

"Did Robert say anything?"

"Nope."

"Well, you never know. No sense worrying about it."

Susan could tell I was worried. "The guy in the book is doing well in Alaska. Maybe we'll call him tomorrow at noon," she joked, hoping to relieve my tension.

"Get the area code," I said.

Wednesday morning came earlier than usual, hurried by a restless night. I went in about 6:30 and spent some extra time with the third shift. After third went off and first came on, I went to my office and closed the door.

I reflected on the last 10 years and especially the last 10 weeks. All in all, it had been a great ride. Lots of hard work and lots of frustration, but it had been worth it. If it had to end, then I knew I'd done my best. The one thing I would regret is never having the opportunity to work for a Charlotte McArthur or Carlton Dallas. Good leaders are rare, and those fortunate enough to have had such a mentor were very lucky indeed.

The phone rang about 9:15. It was Betty from personnel. We had become good friends, sharing inside information when we had it.

Quietly she said, "I had a call from one of my spies up at corporate. He said there are some big things going on, that they had worked late last night and had to come in early this morning. Some early retirement papers are being prepared, and a plant closing announcement is in the works, possibly for today."

At 11:00, another call. It was Amy Stewart, Robert Ellisor's administrative assistant. "The plant manager would like to see you as soon as possible," she said without emotion.

"How's the weather up there?"

"Partly cloudy," she whispered.

As I walked to his office, I thought back to how much I loved baseball when I was growing up. My dad played with me for hours, and I played on an organized team through my freshman year in college. Like most kids, I dreamed of being the hero in a World Series someday.

Right then I felt it was the seventh game, last inning, two outs, bases loaded. There are 70,000 fans screaming like crazy. The Cy Young Award pitcher throws a 94 mile-an-hour fast ball. I hit it just right, and it takes off like a rocket toward the center field fence. The center fielder gracefully goes back with his back against the wall, glove up, and eyes glued on the flight of the ball. The fans go silent, and I am barely running toward first. If the ball stays in, it's an out and I'm the goat. If it goes out of the park three inches past the out-stretched glove, I'm a national hero.

Somehow it doesn't seem right that the difference between victory and defeat—goat and hero—

Courage to Lead

is just three inches. And how about luck, the wind?

On the other hand, it's where I want to be, in the arena. The last few months have been exhilarating with 94-mile-an-hour fast balls every day, and a few curves too, just to keep me on my toes. I have taken my best cut here. I realized that the ball was in the air and out of my control. I'd either be a hero—to my wife anyway—or I'd be a goat. I couldn't think of anything worse than being forced to clean out my desk, pack my stuff, and walk the gauntlet down that long safety lane as all my people stare numbly.

I walked into Robert's office. He did not offer me a chair; I just stood awkwardly on the opposite side of his desk. He said, without smiling, "Jake, I have some good news, and I have some bad news. Which do you want first?"

For some strange reason, all I could think about was where I might find a box big enough for all my stuff.

"Give me the bad news first."

"The bad news is we are going to delay your request for fixing the water cooler."

I thought to myself that the ball had not gone over the fence yet, but if that's the bad news, I may have just dodged the biggest bullet ever shot.

As he pointed to a chair, he said, "The good news is your request for repair of #3 and #4 has been approved, and the replacement for #6 is going out today from corporate. We'll start interviewing immediately to replace your three people."

I said very quietly to no one in particular, "Home run."

"Excuse me?" he asked.

"Oh nothing, I was just thinking out loud."

I was glad he pointed to the chair because my knees had all of a sudden become weak.

He pulled his chair around, took off his glasses and said, "There is more. The plant in Kingston is being closed, and all their work is coming here. Since it's so close geographically, all of their people are being offered jobs here. Also, your boss was offered early retirement this morning. Today is his last day. Carlton instructed me to offer you his job. He wants an answer in three weeks and not before because he wants you to think about it.

"Jake, this is a great opportunity, but it's going to be a lot of work and a lot of pressure. Besides all the people we have here, you'll pick up an additional 45 from Kingston, and a new product being announced this week will require another 30. While all this is going on, the plant will be expanded.

"I don't know what your conversation was with Carlton yesterday, but you obviously said something he liked. The timing is never right on something like this, but we think you are ready. Carlton is a gambler, and he said give you a shot. He very seldom misses the mark."

"This is great news," I said, "but I know he didn't make this decision based on our 15-minute conversation. I know you had a major input, and I appreciate it."

He got up, and as he shut the door, said, "That's true. I was sent here to cut costs and identify the warriors. I have accomplished my job."

"Aren't you going to stick around?"

"Heck no," he responded immediately. "I'm getting outta here on the first boat. I want no part of what's coming up. I'm going back to corporate and count beans where I belong. Frank Morgan, the plant manager at Kingston, is coming here. He's a Carlton Dallas clone and is terrific.

"Besides, Carlton wants me at corporate. I'm one of the few he will listen to, and he needs me to keep him straight. Carlton is smart enough to know he needs to surround himself with people like me."

With great respect for Carlton, he said, "When Carlton gets the corner office on the 47th floor, I'll be right next door.

"Jake, let me tell you something. Everybody knows the story of Carlton Dallas, especially after the newsletter article. But I'll tell you a story, in confidence of course, that I don't think anybody else in the company knows.

"Carlton and I started our careers the same week. We became good friends, maybe because we're so different. I was always interested in administration and accounting. He, of course, was only interested in production. Another reason we became good friends is that we really didn't compete against each other. We worked together in several plants starting out, and we sort of taught each other the things we needed to know to succeed. He is hard-headed with a short attention span, but he's so smart he picks things up very quickly.

"After about six months, corporate sent us up to a charm school in Chicago for entry-level manufacturing managers. It was a week-long conference and really boring. It was in the summer, and he and I would plot to leave as early as we could each day and go sit by the pool and drink piña coladas. After a couple, we would begin to solve all the world's problems, and this would go on until the wee hours.

"He told me something on one of those evenings I haven't heard him mention again, so it's real important that you never divulge this. I just think it's important for you to know the man.

"He said his biggest fear as a Marine officer was to lose people in combat. When he was on the airplane heading to the Mideast, he was not concerned about his own safety, and he was confident he could accomplish the mission. His first priority was to bring all his people home in one piece. He knew the risk, but it was vital to him to get everybody out. As you know, one young Marine died helping him get aboard the helicopter. Carlton couldn't attend the funeral because he was in the hospital fighting for his life.

"When he was discharged in Hawaii, he and his wife flew to California, picked up a car and drove across the country to see the sights. He called ahead to Missouri and arranged to meet the family of the young Marine. The young man had been exceptional: star athlete, all-American kid that every person in the small town knew.

"Carlton went into his parents' home. The young Marine's wife was sitting on the couch with a two-month-old baby and a tightly-folded American flag. He said it was the most gut-wrenching moment of his life to look that family in the eye and say, 'I am the responsible officer.'

"That night in Chicago is the only time in our 20-year friendship I have ever seen him close to becoming emotional. He held himself completely accountable for the loss of that young Marine's life. To this day, the only reminder of his military career is a little plaque behind his desk that says: 'I am the responsible officer.'

"Carlton has told me that so long as he works for Owen, his goal is never to lose the job of a good employee. You know he will terminate non-performers in a minute, but for the true warriors, as he calls them, he will put it all on the line."

Robert got up and walked over to his bookshelf.

"Jake, the board of directors decided about a year ago to close this plant within six months. Carlton had me rewrite the memo, which the president signed off on, to say 'as soon as practical.' That gave him time to work his scheme. He got Frank Morgan and me together and presented his plan. It was for me to come here and squeeze every nickel I could find and assess the personnel. My job was not to make the numbers look good. My job was to make them not look as bad as they were. I never did anything dishonest, but I did use some very creative accounting procedures that were border-line acceptable.

"I told Carlton I would give him one year here and that I didn't think he could pull it off. The board got real antsy with the delays, stalls and excuses. I wouldn't say the shine has disappeared from Carlton's halo, but it sure got a little tarnished.

"His plan was simple, but risky: stonewall it for a year. Carlton figured the economy would turn around, the new product would come out of R&D about the same time, and the jobs would be saved. The board could then take credit for superior stewardship.

"This place has been hemorrhaging money. If it hadn't worked out as it has, and if the board had learned the whole truth, Carlton would have been history, guaranteed. With millions of dollars at stake, the war hero stuff from 20 years ago doesn't mean diddly. He could have closed the plant as instructed, and corporate wouldn't have given it another thought. He literally risked his career for people like Skeeter Lockhart.

"That's the kind of person he is, Jake. Maybe he sees some of that in you. It's a big decision, so think it over real hard."

Robert removed a book from the shelf and returned to his desk.

"Jake, one of the problems we have today is that many individuals, especially those in leadership positions, are unwilling to take responsibility. I hear people every day say, 'I am not a good leader because of my boss, company, spouse, or the economy.' They blame everybody but themselves. Each person has to look inward and take responsibility for productivity and leadership.

"If you do well, as you have, then stand up and take the credit. If you make a mistake, take responsibility and vow to do better next time.

"You have made tremendous progress in the last year, Jake, and especially these last few months. I don't know what Susan has been feeding you, but it has worked."

"Coffee cake and cheesecake," I replied.

Robert smiled broadly, which for him was the equivalent of a belly laugh.

"Robert, I may not get another chance to tell you how much I appreciate what you have done for me personally and what you have done for the people here. You took a big risk, too.

"It's kind of interesting," I continued. "I was talking with a friend recently, and she said when things don't seem to be going well, you must get all the facts before you can make proper judgments, that you have to hear the other side. I take the blame, because I should have pressed for the facts sooner. It may have saved some sleepless nights."

"Well, this is an unusual situation you may never see again," Robert said. "And hopefully one you won't have to see again. We appreciate your stepping up, Jake. Loyalty is not being a 'yes' person; some of the 'yes' people are clearing out their offices today. Loyalty is having the courage to stand up for what you believe." He pointed to a book. "As Thomas Jefferson said, 'One person with courage is a majority.'"

He walked me to the door. As I was leaving, he deadpanned, "Oh, there is one thing Carlton is upset about. If you accept the job, you will be the youngest-ever vice president of production— by one day. He looked it up."

Robert smiled, shook my hand, and returned to his desk.

The announcement came out of corporate precisely at noon. You would have thought our people had all won the lottery, which, in a way, they had. You could tell by their reactions how much they truly cared. It was great to see a year's worth of doubt, frustration, and bitterness begin to subside. It would be very difficult, if not impossible, to get things back where they once were after a year like this. I just wished they could know the whole story, which they never will.

I called Susan several times to tell her the good news, but there was no answer. I figured I would buy some roses on the way home and surprise her.

Thirteen

*A*t about 3:00 I received a call from Charlotte McArthur.

"Jake, I hate like the dickens to bother you, but is it possible for you to run down here at the end of the day for a few minutes? I want to discuss something with you."

I was concerned.

"Are you feeling okay?" That nagging cough had been with her for some time.

"Of course I'm okay. I just have a business op-portunity to tell you about. We don't need an answer immediately, but you do need to be made aware of it so you can think about it. If you can't come until Saturday. . . ."

"Oh, no," I interrupted, "that's fine. I'll be there. I can sneak away a few minutes early and be there by 5:30. I look forward to seeing you."

As she hung up, she said, "Great, I'll have some lemonade ready for you."

I had never made this trip during the week, and it was interesting how different things were. On Saturday you see how people live. During the week you see what they do—tractors, trucks, lots of cars, school kids being discharged from buses with traffic stopped in both directions. The old boys in Wagner were not there, because that was a "Saturday morning thing." The trip took longer than I expected, and I pulled up at Charlotte's about 5:45.

As I walked up to the porch, I put on my "woe is me, I have worked so hard today" look. Charlotte put on her very best sarcastic face and pointed to her watch as if to say, "Great time management."

She laughed and said, "Just kidding, I knew you'd be late. I should have warned you; the traffic this time of day is a real bear. I know you need to get back, so let me get right to the point. And thanks for coming."

She poured some lemonade.

"I sold the company three years ago. There's an old movie with a famous punch line: 'The man made me an offer I couldn't refuse.' That's what happened. It was time anyway. Almost all of our people owned stock in the company. The key people who had worked real hard and stayed there through the tough times made a significant amount, so it was a good deal for all concerned. They made money, kept their jobs and off they went, supposedly to bigger and better things.

"Well, the new people fouled it up. I have always said one of the main reasons companies fail is they stop doing the things that got them to the top. Eastern Airlines, Wang, Wickes, Pan Am, Sears Roebuck, IBM, General Motors, Westinghouse—all were great companies at one time, but they stopped doing the things that made them successful. Some of them you've never heard of because they went out of business about the time you were born. The ones you have heard of are not the giants of their industry they once were.

"The same is true for leaders. You can't get comfortable because somebody out there is always trying to take your place.

"Anyway, the new owners stopped doing the right things. I got a call from one of my key people—please excuse me for saying my company and my people, but that's how I feel. So I get this call about three months ago. It's amazing that you come down here on Saturday and tell me there are some things going on in your company. And the next day my folks call and they're saying pretty much the same things.

"To make a long story short, they have lost business and some especially talented people have quit in disgust. So now the ship is sinking, and they want to sell. What a business deal this would be if I were 20 years younger—I sell the company and three years later I can buy it back for fifty cents on the dollar. Unfortunately, I'm not 20 years younger and can't get involved, except financially.

"Here's the deal. The employees are going to buy it back with some financial help from me. The attorneys and accountants are putting the numbers together now. One of the problems is that there is no one there to run it. All the people I developed are up in years or got mad and quit. I contacted one of the people who would be terrific, but she bought into a small outfit over in New Hope.

"Here is what I have proposed, and they have agreed to—you buy in. The amount it will take is not huge, but it may make your wife a little nervous. They want all the leaders to have a vested interest, and I agree wholeheartedly. Additionally, if at the end of the year everything is going as planned, you will have the option to buy my interest and become CEO. If not, the employees will buy your interest, and we all go our separate ways.

"Jake, this is a great opportunity. I know it's scary and a little risky, but the upside potential is unlimited. The business is still out there, but current management is losing it because of their own blundering. Most of those wonderful people we lost will want to come back. You watch. I'm not gonna call a single one because I'm not going to raid my friends, but when the word gets around, they will call. I've already had one call based on rumor.

"Getting it turned around will require a major effort, but there are some great people out there who would die for the company. The fact that all of them are putting in their own money tells you all you need to know.

"Who knows whether you are ready. I think you are. The technical transition from what you are doing now will be relatively simple. There are risks in everything. But I'm willing to take it, and so are they. The question is, are you? Jake, the decision is yours."

I sat, speechless, and gazed across the lawn into the woods.

She took a sip of lemonade and studied my expression, rocking for a while before she broke the silence.

"Jake, I don't want you for a second to feel your decision will have any impact on what I'm doing. I have committed to help them, so from my perspective, it's a done deal. The people out there are responsible for everything I have. Luckily, because of them I have the resources and quite frankly, I don't see it as much of a gamble. I'm not asking you to do it. It's simply a business opportunity, one of many you'll get in your life-time."

"I'm sure. It's just that this news has come at an awkward time, when so many things are turning around for me at Owen. . . ." I didn't see any need to tell her what had happened that morning.

"Jake, a lot of life is timing, and leaders have to be ready to make big decisions, sometimes in a hurry. Maybe the timing isn't exactly right, but I haven't been involved in anything where everything was just perfect.

"I would like an answer in three weeks. If you would like to look around the plant, which I'm sure you would if you're interested, we can do that anytime. I have the owner's permission to do whatever it takes to get this deal through. I feel sorry for the present owners, but it's a classic case of actions and intentions. They had great intentions, but their actions were totally inconsistent, and it came back to haunt them."

She leaned forward.

"One other thing. You absolutely cannot count on me for anything. I am making no promises, actual or implied. When I walked out the door three years ago, I said I would never go back. It wouldn't have been fair, and I meant it. I still mean it. I'm not going back. It'll be your show, lock, stock and barrel. Do you understand?"

"Yes, I do."

"Okay, I have to meet with the accountants in 15 minutes, so unless you have some questions,

I'll just wait to hear from you."

I was dumbfounded. I was overwhelmed. I had absolutely no questions to ask. There were a thousand things I needed to know, but I honestly could not form the words. I thanked her for everything and left. It seemed the trip back to Callaway took about seven seconds. Getting the flowers for Susan never crossed my mind.

I went straight home. My wife greeted me with surprise.

"What happened to game night?" she asked.

Every Wednesday night most of the managers went down to Pinky's for a beer and a game of backgammon. The rule is as soon as you lose two dollars, you go home. With my complete lack of understanding of the doubling cube, they all took advantage of me and sent me packing pretty early. I was always home by the time the kids went to bed, but rarely this early.

"I decided to skip it this evening."

"Nice to have you home early. How did it go today?" she asked.

"You wouldn't believe it if I told you, which I will when the kids are down."

Dinner was fun. Jake spilled his juice twice, and after a reprimand, Allison posed a thought provoking question, "Mommy, why were you so nice to Mrs. Ward when she spilled her coke on the rug?"

During dinner, I was preparing how I would tell Susan this whole story. It was incredible even to

Charlie Farrell

me that simply asking for directions to a parade could lead where it has. Charlotte talked about luck and how it fits—that all of us have luck, some good and some bad. The key is to capitalize on good luck because you don't get many opportunities like this.

I knew this day would surely be remembered as one of the major turning points in our lives. There would be a lot of trial and tribulation trying to make a decision whether our zip code would be Callaway or Eagle Springs, but just for the moment I wanted to enjoy, to savor, this triumph.

I replayed, in living color, the details of this unbelievable day to Susan. Her eyes welled up and the biggest tear I've ever seen cascaded down her cheek. She was overwhelmed. She, too, could sense the anxiety and frustration of the past year begin to dissolve. And she could see the wonderful opportunity before us.

Her last comment, through teary eyes and the long-absent smile, was, "What a wonderful predicament you have put us in, Mr. Howe."

Fourteen

I always thought a dilemma was a choice between two options, neither of which was acceptable. I don't know what to call a choice between two options, both of which are incredible.

Without the call from Charlotte, I would have been ecstatic because I didn't need three weeks to think it over.

If things hadn't worked out at Owen, I may not have been the happiest man on earth, but I wouldn't have been distraught either. I would have

Charlie Farrell

been happily packing my bags for a short trip down Highway 60.

Susan and I had agreed not to discuss it for a few days. We would try to formulate in our own minds the pluses and minuses of each scenario, and on Friday over a glass of wine we would start to hash it out.

"Well, what do you think?" she began with a big smile. I could tell her happiness quotient was rising.

"What do you think?" I countered.

"I asked first," she said.

"Well, I don't know what to do. I know it's not just a business decision. For the first time in my career, family considerations will have a major impact."

"I was thinking about our last move," Susan said pleasantly. "Moving the kids was so easy. We just bundled them up, got in the car, and headed out. Now with them in school it gets a little more complicated."

"Yeah, it's interesting," I acknowledged. "We have always accepted the fact that with Owen, we would have to move a few times—it was a given. Now that there is an option not to have to move, that given is seen in a different light."

"When would we have to move?" Susan asked.

"No way of knowing for sure, but as you get closer to the top, the picture does get pretty clear. Carlton will be Vice President of Manufacturing for five to ten more years. His next move is president of Owen. Assuming he has his plant managers set, that means I won't have a chance of being a plant manager until he's promoted unless something unforeseen happens. Of course, there's no guarantee that I will ever be a plant manager. With ten plants in the company, the competition is fierce. So the answer to your question, excuse me for rambling, is that we probably move in five to ten years when the kids will be in junior high and high school. The move after that is to the 47th floor in Chicago. How would you like that?"

I love Chicago, and the thought of moving there was exciting to say the least. I knew exactly what Susan's response would be.

"You know me," Susan said, somewhat somber. "I'm a country girl. Callaway is big enough for me, and the idea of being in Eagle Springs in the same house forever with the children in school two blocks away is my idea of heaven.

"Jake, I guess the decision will be based a great deal on what your ultimate business goals are, which we have never really discussed."

"My goal is to run the whole show. In Eagle Springs, that goal is guaranteed in one year. It's a small business compared to Owen, but is not subject to the whims of a board of directors three hundred miles away who have never even visited the plant. But do I want to spend the rest of my life in a small town where everybody knows everything?

"On the other hand, Owen is probably more secure. It is a huge company with deep pockets and working for Frank Morgan, one step away from Carlton Dallas, would be exciting. I am comfortable at Owen. I know the ropes, and I enjoy the confidence of the next president."

"What was her plant like?" Susan asked. I had been down on Thursday to look around.

"Great people—just like Charlotte said. The plant is clean and modern, and the managers and supervisors were eager to meet me and let me know they were excited about the possibility of having me join their company. And, of course, they all think Charlotte is the queen."

As Susan referred to the pros and cons she'd written down, I continued.

"But the people at Owen are great, too. During this past year the adversity has bonded us together, like a team that has fought together and is now victorious. This promotion is because of them, and I would hate to leave after they have done so much. I'm even getting along well with Skeeter."

"How about the pay and benefits?" Susan asked. "I know you well enough that your decision won't be made entirely over the money issue, but I'm sure you've thought about it."

"I have. At Owen, the compensation is more than fair, but now we'd really be getting into the big leagues. The top positions at Owen are the highest paying jobs in the industry, and when you throw in stock options, profit sharing and retirement, it's pretty attractive."

135

Courage to Lead

"And how about McArthur Enterprises?"

"Susan, it's mind-boggling. There we are talking about ownership. Somebody told me once there's a big difference between making a living and making money. I understand now what he meant. At Owen, we would make a darn good living. In Eagle Springs, there's really no limit."

"Jake, you know this decision is ultimately yours. I will continue to give my input, but you'll have to decide. I just know that a lot of your happiness comes from your work, just as most of mine comes from the family. Whether that is right or wrong is beside the point. I have accepted that. And since a lot of our happiness here, as has been proven over the last year, is dependent on your satisfaction with work, it's important that you make a business decision.

"I know you'll consider the family," she continued, "but I don't want you looking back in five years regretting you made your decision simply because of my desires. I'll be happy either way as long as we have our family. I'll support whatever decision you make and not look back . . . even if we are freezing our 'you know whats' off in the Windy City," she concluded with a sly smile.

"You're terrific," I said. "I don't care what the neighbors say about you."

By the next Friday night I was mentally drained. There were still a few days before any answers were due, but I had hit the wall. My mind had turned to mush.

Susan and I decided on Friday night to take a break and not talk about it. After the kids were down, we relaxed. Susan picked up her book on the family in Alaska and continued reading. About 10:00 she gasped, "Oh, no!"

"What happened?" I asked.

Susan, almost in tears, said, "The man was flying out to a logging camp, had a mid-air collision with an eagle and crash-landed into the mountains. He destroyed his airplane, broke his leg and is in a hospital."

"Good thing we didn't call," I said. "Good thing we don't need to. That guy's a leader. Anybody who's done what he has will bounce back. Just keep reading, you'll see."

For the first time in days, I slept soundly. I had a beautiful dream about being in an airliner flying to a tropical paradise. Suddenly, the dream shifted, and I found myself on the beach, in morning sunlight, walking in the surf . . . I had a faint idea that I was searching for something precious, of value, but I was not frantic. Something about the salty air calmed me, and I knew that I would find the prize that had been eluding me. The last thing I remember was looking out on the water and smiling.

I have never believed in the mystical, but it's incredible what the subconscious does while asleep. I went to bed Friday night with a dilemma for which there was absolutely no right answer. I woke

up on Saturday morning with a perfectly clear solution. I wondered why I ever worried about it,
and why I ever considered the alternative. I wanted
to wake Susan up, but she had been going through
this with me, maybe even more with all the risk
involved, so I decided to let her sleep in.

I got up and headed to Eagle Springs. It was
the prettiest Saturday morning ever.

Fifteen

When I got to Wagner, I couldn't resist. I turned into the dusty parking lot of the Starlight Cafe and pulled up close to the three old men drinking their coffee. They had a checkerboard out, and two of them were locked in a do or die battle with the third kibitzing as he saw fit.

"Good morning. How's the coffee here?" I asked.

All three looked up with a smile and the kibitzer said, "Good coffee. Go in and ask Tina or Randy to give you a draw out of the visitors' pot.

Charlie Farrell

You're probably not tough enough to handle the Wagner stuff. If you'd like, come out and join us."

"Thanks, I'll be right back." I went in and ordered as instructed.

Tina just laughed and said, "You'd better look out for those guys. That's a bad crew—a real bad crew."

The Starlight Cafe was filled with folks eating their pancakes, spinning yarns about the big one that got away, and catching up on the price of wheat and soybeans. It was a composite of Wagner—plain folks in a small town striving mightily to resist the invitation to join the 21st century.

I went back outside where they had pulled up a chair for me. All three stood up and introduced themselves: Christopher Preston, Bobby Lucas, and Jack Harden. Charlotte said one of the most important things a leader must do is to remember people's names. You should always answer the phone with a pencil in your hand because the first thing people will say is their name. It's unprofessional to ask at the end of a conversation, "Now, what is your name?"

It's the same with meeting people. For those two seconds when people give their names, give them your total attention, and don't think about what you're going to say. Just listen intently and if you don't get it, ask again. Charlotte says if you can't remember a name 20 seconds later, you didn't forget it, you just never got it. I've been practicing, and I'm getting better: Christopher (as in Columbus), Bobby (as in socks), and Jack (as in-the-box). Got 'em.

"What brings you through here every Saturday morning?" Christopher inquired.

I could tell by the way he asked the question that they were the unofficial clearing house for information on strangers passing through the area. "I'm spending a few Saturday mornings down in Eagle Springs with a friend."

Bobby punched Jack in the ribs and said, with a chuckle, "I bet it's a woman."

"As a matter of fact, it is," I boasted.

They were in their seventies, I guessed, with a lot of miles on their faces—tough, independent, proud. They were the kind of folks that never had much, but what they had was paid for. Chances are two of them had never been out of the county, and the one who had didn't like it.

They were dressed in denim coveralls, plaid long-sleeved flannel shirts, and hats. They were large men who were born out of the fields and ponds of a small farm community.

We chatted casually for awhile. Bobby beat Jack in a game, which cost him a nickel. As Jack disgustedly threw his nickel on the board, Bobby said sarcastically, "About five more years of practice, you'll be pretty good."

As Jack stood up to let Christopher have his seat for the next game, he said to Bobby, "You're so lucky. Don't let that horseshoe in your pocket

fall out and break your foot when you stand up."
They all laughed the laugh which said these men
had a very special friendship going back a long
way.

Christopher looked at Bobby and said to me,
"Jake, why don't you play Bobby a game. He's
really no challenge for me."

Bobby turned his tractor hat around backwards
and said, "Yeah, sit down—I wanna get some of
that city money—you gotta nickel?"

"Yes sir, I do, but I haven't played checkers in
a long time."

Bobby was serious.

"No excuses, young man. If you're gonna play
the game, play the game, but no excuses when
you lose. If I whup ya, so be it. If you whup me,
I'm gonna give you a nickel, shake your hand and
say today you're the better man. Tomorrow may
be a different story, but today, you're the best. I
heard a woman make a speech on that subject a
long time ago—real leaders don't explain and they
don't complain; they just keep playin' the game."

"Oh, who was that?" I asked.

"A woman named Charlotte McArthur from
Eagle Springs."

With that Christopher and Jack threw up their
hands and let out a loud yell.

Christopher exclaimed, "Charlotte McArthur!
Man, I'll never forget the night she came up and
spoke to the Men's Bible Class. You remember
that, Jack?"

Courage to Lead

Jack nodded in amazement at the memory of it all. Chris continued, "I never heard a talk like hers. I'll tell you, she peeled the paint off the walls. Good thing it was all men. She could put blisters on a galvanized tub, but I'll tell you what, friend, she's the best I ever heard."

"I'll never forget the part 'bout being mission-oriented," Jack said. "Leaders don't get up in the morning and ask, 'What am I gonna do today?' They get up in the morning and say, 'This is what I'm gonna do today.' They have a clear-cut mission and direction—in all areas of their life: business, family, health."

Jack swilled his coffee and continued. "I put that idea to work in my business, and it was amazing what it did for our productivity. We all knew from that day forward what we were trying to accomplish.

"Jake, if you went into your business Monday morning and gave 10 people a 3x5 card and asked them to write down the goals of your organization, what do you think they would say?"

"Probably not much," I admitted.

"How do they know their working hours?"

"We tell 'em."

"How do they know the dress code?"

"We tell 'em."

Jack smiled and asked, "Then how are they supposed to know the goals of the organization?"

I was thinking she had taught everybody in the area how to ask those questions. We started playing, and it became clear real quick that my net worth was getting ready to take a beating.

Christopher chimed in. "The thing I remember from that night was how leaders are willing to make decisions. It kills productivity and enthusiasm when highly-paid individuals will not make a 50-cent decision. Set a date to make the decision and make it. She said in most cases it's better to make the wrong decision quickly than no decision at all. By waiting there is no guarantee that you will make a better decision, and once you find out you've made a bad decision, you can change it and make it right. She really is something."

Chris waved at a passer-by and said, "I called her a couple weeks later and asked her to help out with a project. She said she really appreciated me asking, but if it didn't have something to do with her business or family, she really wasn't interested. She didn't make excuses, nothing about lack of time. She just said if it's not family or business, she wasn't interested. You can't help but admire her honesty."

Jack jumped in. "I liked the part about how some things change, but some things never do. Jake, have you ever heard of VCR's, cellular phones, PC's, fax machines, or microwave ovens?"

"I've heard of fax machines, but I don't know what they do."

"Well, all of these were hot items in every home and business back when you were running around in diapers. Now they are obsolete or have been updated so many times they're called something different. Voice was transmitted over ugly wires strung up and down the road, and everybody was polluting the air with gasoline powered cars.

"All of that has changed. What has not changed are the principles of leadership. They are eternal.

"She even quoted some ancient Chinese warrior, Kung Fu or Sun Fu, who was riding around on a horse 2,000 years ago spouting principles of leadership that modern day writers claim as their own.

"Don't get wrapped up in the technical stuff, Jake, and lose sight that people are the essence of leadership. Heck, some folks know more about their products than they do about the people that build, sell, and buy 'em."

As he picked up the last checker in victory, Bobby proudly declared, "I was president of the Bible Class at the time. I got to introduce her. After her speech was over, we gave her a beautiful pen and pencil set, just like the one you have in your shirt pocket, Jake. She said it was the only one like it she had ever seen—I picked it out myself."

I took out a nickel and offered it to Bobby. "You're the better man. I've enjoyed meeting you folks, but I'd better get on down the highway."

Bobby put up his hand in protest. "Keep your nickel. Put it up on a shelf where you can see it. When you look at it, just remember one thing: don't bet money with strangers in a game you don't understand. That will keep you out of financial trouble the rest of your life." With a big grin, he pronounced, "You see, Chris and Jack here are the number two and three ranked checker players in the world!"

Jack offered a leathery hand and said, "Tell your lady friend in Eagle Springs the three barons of Wagner send their regards."

"You can bet I will," I assured him.

As I walked toward the car, the battle continued: three warriors, three friends, three gentlemen.

Driving to Eagle Springs, I thought about Christopher's comment—how Charlotte had said no to anything but family and business. It made me wonder why she had spent so much time with me. I'm not family, and until this week, there wasn't a business connection. I hadn't thought about it until then, but it did seem strange.

I pulled into the driveway. Her car was not there, but a note was tacked to the front door. The note said, "Come in and read the letter by the chair." Next to the letter was a thermos of hot coffee. I opened the envelope. There were several handwritten pages folded around an old photograph and Charlotte's gold sand dollar.

Sixteen

*D*ear Jake,

There is cheesecake in the refrigerator. Help
yourself. When you're done, just leave the dishes
on the table. Gladys has a key, and I have asked
her to come over and clean up. If you are like
most men, you couldn't even find the dishwasher,
much less figure out how to operate it. It's not
that I don't trust you, but I'm not taking any
chances.

I don't know exactly where to begin or where

this is going, so I will just start and try to put all my thoughts on paper. If I ramble, please excuse me.

I was born into a middle class family of loving parents, who, like most parents, spoiled me as an only child. I got all the attention and was given anything I wanted materially. I never caused my parents any problems, but I didn't really appreciate, until much later, all the things I had and how much my parents taught me. I was especially close to my mother. When I finished high school, I had no aspirations for college.

About that time, my father's business was caught in a recession and money was real tight. I left home with a girlfriend and moved to southern California. It was a fun and exciting time. We had a little apartment on the beach in Corona del Mar, and I held a series of odd jobs to make what little money I needed.

After a couple of years, my lifestyle was starting to get old, and I couldn't see much of a future. I hadn't met any guys that I really liked, so I had nothing to keep me there. I even started to think about going home to attend college.

I was alone walking on the beach one beautiful Sunday morning when I met a fellow coming from the opposite direction. We were the only two out that early, and we chatted casually for a few seconds about the nice weather. Both of us continued our walks in opposite directions. A few seconds after we parted, we both turned around to look and had that rather embarrassing, unmistakable eye contact that said, "I'm attracted to you." We both turned away and continued walking.

I was drawn to this stranger. He was handsome and strong but somewhat shy. I could tell he was ill at ease meeting someone in that way, but his easy-going manner charmed me. I guess neither one of us could think fast enough to come up with a line to keep the conversation going. His dark eyes had a mischievous sparkle, and his sincere manner was immediately infectious.

I was a waitress at The Galley, a small cafe in the marina. I kept hoping maybe by chance he would show up for lunch one day, but no such luck. I knew by the end of the week what I was going to do Sunday.

I got up at first light, fixed myself up and headed to the beach. For some reason I knew he would be there, and he was. We met again in about the same spot. We introduced ourselves this time— playing those games of where are you from, what do you do, how long have you been here? If there was ever a case of instant magnetism, that was it.

He came to the cafe on Tuesday for lunch, and I even remember what he ordered: a fried grouper sandwich with clam chowder and iced tea. He asked me to go to a movie with him that night after work, and I was so excited I could hardly work. He was the first man I had met with any real substance.

We had a whirlwind courtship, and he asked

me to marry him exactly 36 days and three hours after we met. His name was Jacob James Howe—your father. We were on the beach where we met when he proposed. As we were walking in the surf, I spotted a sand dollar and picked it up.

Jake, I suspect right now you are in shock. I can assure you that the mix of emotions you are experiencing pales in comparison to the joy and fear I have felt over the last three months.

I can never explain the love and admiration I had for your father. He was, as you know, brilliant, honest and hard-working. The early days of our marriage were the most wonderful of my life. He was the first man I ever loved. As you know, loving someone and being in love are two different things. We had both.

You were born two years to the day after our wedding. I'll never forget his laugh when he said, "What a bummer—we're never going to be alone on our anniversary because of Jake's birthday." When he came to take us home from the hospital, he brought the sand dollar we had found. He had taken it to a jeweler and had it gold plated. It has been around my neck since that day.

Unfortunately, before you were born, our marriage started to falter. The reasons were many, none of which had to do with you. I guess it was a combination of my immaturity and his stubbornness.

You were the joy of our lives, but we could never rekindle the passion and devotion of the early days of our marriage. We made the decision to separate. I lacked any formal education and had no way of supporting you. He, of course, was doing well with a great job and a bright future. We decided that you would stay with him. Under the circumstances, it was the right decision.

We made a hasty choice grounded in the anger we felt toward each other. I was too young to understand the anguish and guilt I would carry with me, but both of us were quite sure we never wanted to see each other again. However, as time passed, especially when my girls were born, what we did became a tremendous burden. Your father, in an obvious effort not to discredit me, never told you the true story. I know now your father's actions were honorable.

I've never believed in living in the past. Looking for solutions and opportunities is impossible while looking backward. When it's over, it's over, and no amount of talking will change or erase it.

I have made a ton of mistakes in my life, and I was pretty good at letting them go and not looking back. But this is one which I never let go. I tried to get in touch with your dad several times, but you two had just left Kansas for what I know now was Virginia. Then I got married and had my girls. Living in a small town where my husband grew up, I felt revealing my past could only hurt. Wilson was the only one who knew.

I have gone to find your dad. I don't know where he is, but I will find him. I want, if nothing else,

Charlie Farrell

to tell him thank you for the wonderful job he did bringing you up.

I suspect you don't fully appreciate what he's done for you. He raised you, taught you how to play baseball, and instilled in you a wonderful set of values. Your honesty and work ethic are without equal. He worked hard, sacrificing his personal life to put you through college, and I am quite certain he sacrificed his professional career as well. While his peers were going off to school and working late to get ahead, he chose to be with you. I am sad you don't have the relationship with him that you should.

As you know, I have not been feeling well. I was diagnosed three years ago with a serious illness. That's why I sold the company. Through treatment, the disease was put into remission, but the cough you noticed is the telltale sign it has returned. I put off going to the doctor until this week because of all the things going on with the company, but I knew it wouldn't make any difference. The doctor warned me that if the disease returned at my age, there was no hope. I was told I have between six months and a year.

I'm not giving up. Doctors have been wrong before, and they are surprised that I have done so well the last three years. But I have to be realistic, too. At some time or another the curtain must come down. If this is my time, so be it. I have had the most wonderful life imaginable, capped off on April 21 of this year when you said, "My name is Jake

Howe."

When I find your dad and make things right, I will gladly go with a smile on my face. I have only one wish before then—for the three of us to spend just five minutes together—to cry, to hug, and to share. There is a precious piece of all our lives that is missing. The only way to fix it is to find the man I loved a long time ago. I still love him. I just didn't realize it until you came back into my life.

I have struggled with the thought of telling you all this, that maybe under the circumstances after all these years it would be best for you not to know. My decision to tell you this is based on our conversation about the "piece that was missing." Almost all great leaders have mentioned a closeness to one or both of their parents. You never had that, and it was apparent. Now, you can.

No one else knows of this letter, so I will leave it up to you what you want to divulge. As you know, my girls have moved away and are doing well in their own lives. At this point, it doesn't matter to me who knows.

My attorney, Ross Crane, has the papers on the buyout of the business. The money is in escrow, and he has the power of attorney to act in my behalf. In the event of my death, my share of the company will be sold to you for $1. In this way, you become an equal partner in my estate, which you deserve. My attorney thought this rather strange, but I have done stranger things, and he knows better than to ask me why. In this way you get what is rightfully yours, and no one has to know. He also has copies of your birth certificate and the marriage license of Charlotte Riggins and Jacob Howe.

The picture is of you and me on your fourth birthday. The pony's name was Sheeba. I can still feel the big hug you gave me at the end of that day. I've never seen anyone as excited.

The sand dollar is for you. Put it in a safe place, or give it to Susan. It has worked miracles for me, and it will for you. I'm not an overly religious person, but the last thing I did every night for the last 35 years is hold the gold sand dollar and pray that you were safe. My prayers have been answered.

I learned a long time ago that true happiness is someone to love, something to do, and something to look forward to. Those three things have been missing in my life, but now, thanks to you, I have them back. I am on a mission, and now I must go. Time is precious.

I fully expect to see you soon. If for some reason I don't, I want you to know how much I love you as my son and admire you as a person. If I could ever have written a script for how I wanted you to turn out, you have exceeded my expectations many times over.

I will love you forever,

Mom

Seventeen

*M*onday morning, and it was 8:15. I'd had my coffee and Hannibal was doing his thing. After all the recent announcements, the morale of the people was unbelievable. I walked up to Robert Ellisor's office and looked in. He was going over the numbers as usual, but he looked relaxed for the first time in a year. Cheerfully, he said, "Good morning, Jake, how was your week-end?"

"Really good, Robert, thanks. Things are going great in my department. The adrenaline that's flowing will keep them going for at least another week, and all I could do is get in the way. I have some vacation time built up, and Carlton said he didn't want an answer yet, so I thought I would get away for awhile and think it over."

"That's great, Jake. You deserve it. Why don't you take off now, and I'll let personnel know. Have a good time and give my regards to Susan."

"Thanks a lot. I'll grab some stuff from the office and head out." I returned to my office, got out the phone book and looked up the number of Travel Unlimited. "May I speak to Hilda?"

"Sure, just a moment."

"This is Hilda. May I help you?"

"Good morning, Hilda. This is Jake Howe over at Owen. I would like a round-trip ticket to Key West, Florida."

WOODY COBBS